Margaret Mitchell: A Scarlett or a Melanie

ISBN-13: 978-0-9846347-9-8
ISBN-10: 0-9846347-9-7

First printing: September, 2012

Cover and title page photographs of Scarlett and Melanie furnished by David O. Selznick, used with permission.

Published by:

 tm

ThomasMax Publishing
P.O. Box 250054
Atlanta, GA 30325
404-794-6588
www.thomasmax.com

Margaret Mitchell: A Scarlett or a Melanie

Susan Myrick

edited by Susan Lindsley

ThomasMax

Your Publisher
For The 21st Century

A WORD FROM THE PUBLISHER

You are reading one of two prize-winning entries from the 2012 ThomasMax "You Are Published" Contest, which is held annually in conjunction with the Southeastern Writers Association's annual conference and workshop held each June. This is not a self-published work, but rather one chosen from numerous contest entries. The award has been given since 2006. No award was given in 2011, as the winner had to decline because she was under contract to an agency. Previous winners include:

Randall Arnold, *The Resemblance*, 2006
Martha Ruth Phillips, *Written on a Rock*, 2007
Kathleen McKenzie, *Principal Murder*, 2008
Judith Barban, *Poplar River*, 2009
Grace Walker Looper, *Southern Fire*, 2010
Frances Ruffin, *Famiglia*, 2012

If you are a writer and would like to submit your book to our annual contest, plan to attend the SWA Workshop (only workshop attendees are eligible). There are other contests as well with cash prizes. Information can be found at www.southeasternwriters.com. More information on our contest can be found at our publisher website at www.thomasmax.com/contest.htm. You can find guidelines there.

The SWA Workshop is one of the finest educational and social experiences a writer or aspiring writer can have. Not only do attendees receive instruction from experts in various writing fields, the four-day affair is held in a sequestered environment where writers, instructors and board members get to know each other personally as well as networking for professional reasons. Our personal opinion is it's the best time a writer can have and keep his/her clothes on!

Lee Clevenger and R. Preston Ward, ThomasMax Publishing

(Contest is subject to discontinuation at any time)

WORDS FROM THE EDITOR

This book is a collection of articles Susan Myrick wrote over the years about her friend Peggy Mitchell and *Gone With the Wind*, both the book and the movie, and contains three feature articles about survivors of the War Between the States. The title article was prepared in 1983 by the editor from Sue's diary and from her notes on an article she had begun.

Except for the title article, the stories about Mitchell and GWTW are given in chronological order. There is some repetition, especially in the two reviews of Richard Harwell's book *Margaret Mitchell's* Gone With the Wind *Letters*. All articles are included in full because, in spite of the repetition, each one stands alone and contains some information written (or delivered) for different audiences.

ACKNOWLEDGMENTS

This book would never have been possible without the on-going support of my life partner Gail Cabisius and my two sisters, Lil James and Thulia Bramlett. Thanks, gals, for all the time and effort you gave to this book.

Several individuals provided illustrations for this book. Sybil Fowler and Carolyn Fowler Smith, the picture of Confederate veteran Algernon Sidney Tennille; David Seibert, the pictures of Liberty Hall and the Crawford Long birthplace; and William (Benny) Hawthorne, the picture of the Jackson sisters.

Thanks also to the *Macon Telegraph*, *Southern Living*, the Georgia Historical Society, the Atlanta Public Library and the *Georgia Review* for use of Sue's articles they had published.

And special thanks to John Wiley, Jr., for supplying copies of the "lost columns" Sue wrote while in Hollywood.

-- Susan Lindsley

*For
the
Windies*

TABLE OF CONTENTS

MARGARET MITCHELL:
A SCARLETT OR A MELANIE?

What was Margaret Mitchell really like? Was she a Scarlett as many have said, or was she a Melanie, as others have said? She laughed heartily when she first heard somebody say she was a Melanie; she snorted when somebody first called her a Scarlett. She would say:

Scarlett was NOT me. Nor was Melanie. In fact, nobody in Gone With the Wind *is real. They are all people of my imagination.*

The world knows that Margaret Mitchell was a "private person." She refused to autograph books. She did not answer her phone when thousands of persons called to ask if Rhett ever went back to Scarlett. She stayed at home and wore last year's clothes rather than face the strangers who tried to mob her on Peachtree Street or in the shop where she might be trying to select a hat. She refused to have anything at all to do with the making of the movie and never offered any suggestions as to whom she would like to have play Rhett or Scarlett or Belle Watling.

In one of the many letters to me she wrote:

I had a truly dreadful time yesterday downtown. I wanted to buy chintz for a slip cover and I went to three stores to get away from people. I got no chintz but I did get fallen arches as I stood for hours, mainly listening to Charleston people howling about Clark Gable and demanding that Basil Rathbone be given the part. I finally said, 'So, South Carolina is still fighting lost causes,' and lit a shuck. (See Appendix I.)

Though I had known Peggy Marsh for a long time and had spent many delightful weekends visiting her in the apartment where she and her husband, John Marsh, lived, and of course knew she was writing a book, she never talked to me about it. When, one day, I said: "Peggy, I wish you would let me read some of that book you are reported to be writing," she replied, "I'd just as soon walk naked down Peachtree Street as to let anybody see that manuscript."

Those of us who knew her well for years knew her as a charming, witty, bright, delightful person who told the best stories in the world. We knew that she had certain reticences and we respected her wishes, but anyone who tried to get her to talk about things she did not wish to discuss quickly found that she was obstinate in her desire to keep her private life a private affair.

Like Melanie, Margaret Mitchell was kind and understanding, compassionate and gentle. Like Scarlett, she was immensely attractive, plucky, and unyielding (when she wanted to be). Like both of her characters, she had spunk and backbone.

Like Melanie, she was always polite; she possessed and believed in the good manners of the Old South. Like Melanie, she was unswerving in her loyalty to the South, to the Confederacy, to Lee and Davis and the Confederate Cause. She was of the Old South, yet she was a part of the Jazz Era.

In her young womanhood, she was an ardent admirer of Scott Fitzgerald's writings; she might have been one of his characters in her appeal to men in her femininity, in her breaking away from the "genteel behavior" of the Nineties. She made her debut at the Driving Club and was one of the most popular dancers. She did not hesitate to perform an Apache Dance, to the delight of her audience. Going, as a reporter for *The Atlanta Journal*, to interview Gutzon Borglum who was carving a tribute to the Confederacy on Stone Mountain, she rode in a bosun's chair, dressed in coveralls. For a picture to go with a story she wrote about a circus, she was lifted atop the elephant by its trunk. She climbed a scaffold to get a story about how a man painted a house. By some of the old-fashioned of Atlanta, she was regarded as a tomboy.

Margaret Mitchell did not climb a ladder to show off, nor ride a bosun's chair to cause talk. She had a passion for truth in reporting and she wanted to know the facts before she told her story.

Her passion for accuracy in reporting is what made *Gone With the Wind* historically correct in every way. She spent, as the world knows, thousands of hours in research so that stories she had heard and tales told of the Confederate soldiers in the War Between the States would be provable. Every detail of the history of the period was carefully studied and proven for her personal demands.

That passion for accuracy was the reason she put so much stock in how Southern houses appeared in the movie made from her novel. That was why she was so disturbed over Producer Selznick's insistence on making Tara look like the capitol at Montgomery or a house on the Natchez Trail. She wrote to me:

I grieve to hear that Tara has columns. Of course it didn't and looked nice and ugly like Alexander Stephens' Liberty Hall and the birthplace of Doctor Crawford Long at Danielsville. (See Appendix II.) *Of course, I shall have to state in answer to questions (when the picture is released) that Tara is all wrong and never had any columns at all. I know I will be asked this question seven million times and by seven thousand papers because it is the favorite question I am asked, next to "Did she get him back?"*

That passion for accuracy was what made her write me:

Hooray for you for keeping cotton out of the front yard at Tara. What will they think of next? Probably cotton on the front porch at Tara like porch-cotton Crackers. And three cheers for your taking the English riding britches off Gerald. You know no Irishman would wear English-cut pants. I hope you win your battle against the pink bows on the pickaninnies' hair.

I had thought for two years I would go to Hollywood to serve as technical adviser on customs and manners and speech of the Old South, although no contract had been signed. During those months, Margaret Mitchell and I had many visits together and I asked many questions about things I felt a little doubtful about. I had read the book carefully, marking sentences that I felt would sustain my attitudes on manners, customs and speech, and when Peggy and I would talk far into the night, she would give her opinions of various matters. But she did not forget her statement to Selznick that she would have nothing to do with the movie. Even as well as I knew her, I was constantly surprised at her replies to questions. She often said, "Don't quote me when you get to Hollywood, and after you are there, don't ever ask me anything."

On one occasion on the Hollywood set, there was an argument between Director Fleming and Vivien Leigh about how Scarlett would behave in a certain scene. Everything stopped while Vivien went to her dressing room and Fleming stalked off the set. For hours no camera was turned, no scenes were shot. Miss Leigh's maid came to me and said Miss Leigh would like to talk to me. When I got to her dressing room, she wanted to know if I agreed with her, and I told her I was not employed to interpret the script. She wanted me to call Miss Mitchell to ask what SHE thought.

I refused. Mr. Selznick sent for me and wanted me to phone Peggy.

Again, I refused, politely, and told Mr. Selznick she had asked me not to ask her anything at all about the movie making as she had sworn not to have anything to do with it. Later, Mr. Selznick phoned her. She refused to discuss the matter with him.

Yes, Peggy could be stubborn—as stubborn as Scarlett or Rhett. She stuck to her word to Selznick when she sold him the movie rights—she would have nothing to do with making the movie.

A facet of her personality was her refusal to permit the use of her name in any sort of advertisement. She wrote me:

Please tell Mr. Selznick and the Publicity Department that under no circumstances will I permit them to quote my remarks about your newspaper articles in their promotion program. During the past three years whenever I have voiced an honest and enthusiastic opinion about anybody's writing, I have been in danger of immediately getting a request to use my statement for advertising, and I have had frequent experiences of this kind about newspaper stories.

I'm not exaggerating when I tell you that requests for statements about books, magazine articles and newspaper stories have run into the thousands. I've had to turn them all down, even at the risk of appearing most ungenerous and ungracious, but I did not intend to have my name appearing six times a day in newspapers recommending this or that. I might as well go ahead and endorse Pond's Cold Cream and get it over with, and I have no intention of doing that sort of thing.

To make matters worse there would be the unavoidable suspicion that Mr. Selznick had paid for the use of my name. This would give a number of people a chance to say that as long as I got paid for the use of my name, I did not care how it was used.

In 1937, I sent Peggy a clipping from the *New York Post* which a New York friend had sent me. She wrote to thank me for it and went on to say:

Some of it made me so mad I nearly broke an artery—the gentleman who was so reticent about giving his name (and he SHOULD be reticent) quoted me as saying a number of things I never said. This included statements such as the amount of John's salary, how much I loved him, and now nicely he had supported me for eleven years. As I would not discuss such things with a close friend, I would not be likely to unburden myself on a stranger in this chummy manner. The whole quotation was so cheap and seemed to make me guilty of poor taste.

These statements of Peggy's give a good impression of what sort of woman she was. Only she herself, and her family and most intimate friends can conceive of the thousands of obnoxious references to her personal life she had to endure. Reading Margaret Mitchell's published letters gives an idea of what she lived through, but it is impossible to know the full measure of untruths that were published about this author who only wanted to be left alone.

To her friends she was generous with praise, and to all who made a gesture toward complimenting her on the novel, she was meticulous in her expressed thanks. But she was like a mother with a favorite child whom someone had called ugly or dummy or simple; she would leap "like a duck on a June bug" on anyone who falsely belittled her novel.

Of her novel she said to me once,

It had taken me ten years to weave it as tight as a silk pocket handkerchief. If one thread were broken or pulled, an ugly ravel would show through clear to the other side of the material.

So it was that she was sick at heart at having a Tara that was not true to the section of Georgia about which she wrote, nor to the O'Hara family, but looked more like the Savannah homes of the sort from which Scarlett's mother came.

Perhaps the greatest thing about Miss Mitchell's book is her close weaving of the pocket handkerchief so that it is true to Southern beliefs and Southern history.

One day on the set at Selznick's Forty Acres, I talked with the famous Negro Choir Director Hall Johnson whose group sang in the scene of GWTW that depicted the final days of the siege of Atlanta by Sherman's troops. He talked of his ideas of the music for the background of the movie. I wrote Mr. Selznick a note and said I liked Johnson's idea and I should be glad if he would talk with Hall on the matter. Mr. Selznick wrote me in return that he had been considering Hall for the job but he added: "I understand Miss Mitchell objected strenuously to having Negroes singing as background for this picture. Will you check that for me?"

I replied that her objections were not against Negroes singing but against having Negro field hands at Tara suddenly burst into music on the front lawn at Tara, but I felt certain she would not object to Johnson's choir as an unseen background, much as they had sung in *Green Pastures*, although in the stage production they were more closely related to the movement of the play than they would be in GWTW. I wrote Peggy what I had told Selznick.

She replied that she got a good laugh out of his memorandum to me that she objected to the Negroes singing, and that he was utterly wrong about it. She and her husband, she said, were sick to nausea at seeing the combined Tuskegee and Fisk Jubilee Choirs bounce out at the most inopportune times and in the most inopportune places and sing loud enough to split the eardrums. She objected, she admitted, to that and to the waving of several hundred pairs of hands with Rouben Mamoulian shadows leaping on the walls.

This was fine and fitting in "Porgy" but pretty awful in other shows where it had no place.

She added that she had feared three hundred massed Negro singers might be standing on Miss Pittypat's lawn and singing "Swing Low, Sweet Chariot" when Rhett drives up with the wagon to take Scarlett back to Tara.

Miss Mitchell and her husband always fought for Negro education and even when they were at their worst financially they helped keep Negro children in schools, furnishing car fare and clothes. She even told me once of the "terrible hours" when she had to help with homework that dealt with fractions. She paid for medical care and on many occasions nursed sick Negroes. She told me that the Negroes of Atlanta had nothing but nice things to say about her novel.

The Negro press, she said, considered her book an insult to the race because she had various characters use the term "Nigger" and "darkey," regardless of the fact that nice people in antebellum days called them "darkies." She wondered, she said, if they thought she should have referred to them as "race members."

There are Professional Negroes just as there are Professional Southerners and, from what I can learn from Negroes I have talked to, they are no more beloved by their race than Professional Southerners are by us.

Long before the book or the movie, Peggy and her husband were the most sought-after persons at the Press Institute meetings. I remember her description of the evening at the old Georgian Hotel in Athens, when the Georgia Press Institute meeting was underway:

The people sitting on the beds you wouldn't believe. As more people came into the room, those farthest back on the beds moved still farther back until somebody was sitting on the floor behind the bed; by

11 o'clock goodness knows how many were on the floor. And the spray from the ginger ale bottles and the sparkling water mixers was as thick as that over the Maid of the Mist at Niagara Falls.

On the floor sat gray-haired editors of small town weeklies, young reporters from Macon, Atlanta, Augusta, and Columbus, state editors, writers of bridge columns, and even University of Georgia professors and journalism teachers—all eyes fastened on Peggy, everybody listening raptly to the riotously exaggerated stories she told.

Waves of laughter rolled over the room, splattered against the walls and swept out through the open door in the hallway. John Marsh sat beside his wife, looking admiringly at her, laughing with the audience and giving the word to all that she was the funniest thing in the whole world.

Truly a woman of many facets, Peggy Mitchell was therefore both a Melanie and a Scarlett; she was a loveable, admirable woman, true to her convictions and determined to present a true picture of the South "be-fo' de Wah" and of the vicissitudes of the Southerners during "de Wah" and during the tragic era of Reconstruction. Never has a better picture been given of those times than in her novel.

Georgia Journal, February/March 1983

Editor's Note: Sue often told her niece Lil Lindsley James that Peggy Mitchell was the life of any party, and then asked: "Would you want to go to a party with Scarlett or Melanie?"

Sue also told her niece Susan Lindsley about Mitchell using much of her GWTW money for full scholarships for young black men to attend Morehouse College in Atlanta and also to attend medical school. This Mitchell "secret" has recently been publicized by Ambassador Andrew Young in his TV documentary "Change in the Wind."

PARDON MY UN-SOUTHERN ACCENT

"Fiddle-dee-dee! There hasn't been any fun at any party this spring."

Vivien Leigh, dressed in a green-flowered muslin that billowed its twelve yards of softness over her hoops, talked to the Tarleton twins on Tara's front porch—a make-believe Tara that was only a shell of a house on Forty Acres at Selznick International Pictures in Culver City. The vivacious English actress was rehearsing the first scene of *Gone With the Wind*. She looked just as Scarlett O'Hara should look: her chin was pointed, her eyes reflected the green of the ribbons that fluttered at her breast, her skin was magnolia-white and she lowered her black lashes and pouted her lips in accordance with the traditions of Southern flirtatiousness. The director and the cameraman looked pleased. David O. Selznick looked divinely happy. But I was worried.

I had been engaged as technical adviser on accent, manners and customs for the movie, and my Georgia ears caught something wrong with Scarlett's speech.

I repeated the line half aloud, using my native Georgia tongue:

"Theah hasn't been any fun at any pahdy—"

Ah! I had it. Vivien Leigh was saying "pahty," and Scarlett O'Hara would say "pahdy."

We rehearsed the line again, this time with Vivien pronouncing the *t* as if it were a *d*. The take was made. I nodded in response to the director's questioning look, as I was to do many more times during the six-months filming of Margaret Mitchell's best seller.

When David O. Selznick first asked me to serve as technical adviser, my friends sighed with envy. "Imagine teaching Clark Gable," they said. But I was scared. The job of putting the South in the mouth of an outsider frightened me more than the entrance of the Yankees into Atlanta scared the Confederate ladies.

I had heard many of my friends in Georgia groan and I had seen them tear their hair as they listened to the phony Southern accents of pseudo residents of my old Kentucky home at the movies. I had seen the more sensitive of my acquaintances walk out of the dark theater, shuddering violently as imitation Southerners drawled such phrases as:

"Honey chile, you all sho' are mighty sweet an' I cain't stan' it if you all don' stop bein' so nice to me."

Mr. Selznick was on the spot. He had received countless letters telling him how Southerners should talk and how they should not talk; thousands of residents of the Deep South had begged that no "you alls" should be in the picture; hundreds of them who lived South of the Mason-Dixon line had besought no drawling; and wires, letters and telephone calls by the hundreds had told Mr. Selznick that no British Vivien Leigh could ever sound like a Southern girl.

"Why should an English girl get the role of Scarlett O'Hara, anyway?" demanded enraged loyal Southerners. "Why wasn't a Southern girl good enough for the part?"

"We'll boycott the picture if the accent is not right," they stormed.

Charlestonians had written well-bred, courteously phrased, dignified letters, insinuating that Rhett Butler must sound like a real Charlestonian or Fort Sumter might be fired upon again.

The storm over the choice of an English actress for Scarlett had been lulled a bit when Mrs. E. Dorothy Blount Lamar, President-General of the United Daughters of the Confederacy, and Margaret Mitchell issued statements that Georgians of 1860 probably talked a good deal more like Britishers of today than like the Midwesterners of the United States of the present time; or, for that matter, like anyone in the United States not reared in the South. But other letters pooh-poohed the idea of an English accent that resembled the Southern speech. One man wrote:

"English accent and Southern accent are just as different as Ptomaine Tommy's place on North Broadway is different from the Brown Derby. Southern accent is forty per cent plain cornfield Nigger. I am a damned fool to be taking up my time giving advice not asked for, but somebody has made a mistake which should be corrected before it is too late."

Now, I know that nothing makes the Southerner so red with rage as the insinuation that he talks like a Negro. As long ago as 1842 such a statement was made by Charles Dickens, who wrote home when he was visiting in the United States.

"All the women who have been bred in slave states speak more or less like Negroes from having been constantly in childhood with black nurses."

Nearly a hundred years later your Southerner still grows violently angry over the statement, and he quotes such notables as William Cabell Greet of Barnard College and Cleanth Brooks of Louisiana State, who have taken great pains to refute the statement. Dr. Greet says:

"When the slaves were brought to America they learned the accent of their masters. There is literally no pronunciation among Negroes, with the possible exception in Gullah, that does not occur generally in vulgar or old-fashioned American speech."

And Brooks adds: "In almost every case the specifically Negro forms turn out to be older English forms which the Negro must have taken originally from the white man and which he retained after the white man had begun to lose them."

So, I argued, unless Mr. Selznick wanted the whole South at his throat he'd better not have it said the white characters in *Gone With the Wind* talked like Negroes, and if he didn't want a riot squad for protection at the Atlanta première he'd better not have Olivia de Havilland, Vivien Leigh, Clark Gable and Leslie Howard talk as the average Yankee thinks the Southerner talks.

Frankly, then, we agreed that the white folks in the picture should use a speech suggestive of the South, a sort of denationalized accent akin to that of an educated Middle-Georgian.

We would use the soft *r* and those localisms in which Margaret Mitchell's novel abounds. Ladies who deviated from the code of etiquette of the Sixties would be known as "fast"; perfume would be "Florida water"; the evening meal would be, not dinner, but supper; Mother and Father would be Ma and Pa; an unfashionable gown would be "tacky"; and an impertinent child would be "uppity."

There would be no "you alls" when one person was meant (though we know we Southerners will never rid outsiders of the belief that we do use the words in the singular); there would be no dropped consonants and nobody would pronounce the singular first person pronoun as if it were spelled "Ah."

There would be no drawling. Your Southerner does not drawl, say speech authorities. He actually speaks as many words per minute as does any person from other sections of the United States. The effect of a drawl is produced by a slight lengthening of the first part of a word. He seems to make two syllables of a one-syllable word and to elongate the first syllable. Your usual American says "stor-re": your Britisher says "stoah," and your Southerner, "sto-ah," lingering slightly on the first part of the word.

The speech for all the whites (except Belle Watling, po'whites and Yankees) would resemble the cultured speech of the lowland Southerner as distinguished from that of the tidewater Southerner, who puts broad *a*'s in many words (only to change, for no seeming reason, and pronounce the *a* in Pa and Ma as if it were the *a* in hat), and includes *y* before *a*, *i* or *o* (as cyard, Cyarter, cyow, kyind).

Clark Gable had a Midwestern accent, pronouncing his *r*'s as if they were twins, so he was set to practicing: "I can't afford a four-door Ford though I wish I could afford forty-four four-door Fords." He was warned, too, that some hotheaded son of a Confederate would be ready to put a load of buckshot into a handsome actor's leg if Rhett Butler said "fo-do' " instead of "fo-ah-do-ah."

But Clark had occasional trouble with Southern words, the worst probably in the scene where Rhett Butler presents the green bonnet to Scarlett and teasingly reproaches her for accepting it; "A lady may accept from a man only such gifts as books and flowers and Florida water."

Now, Mr. Gable naturally pronounces Florida as if he was adding *da* to the name Flora, while your Georgian calls the state just south of his own "Florida," to rhyme with "corrida," but what the South calls "wawteh" Gable calls "watter." So Gable, who seldom forgets a line and spoils few takes by blowing scenes, almost met his Gettysburg from "Florida wawteh." I think we made that scene twenty-five times!

With Vivien Leigh and Leslie Howard the problem of Southern speech was more complicated. The most important difference between British and American accent lies not in pronunciation but in intonation, says Dr. R. J. Menner of Yale; and H.L. Mencken says, "In general the speech tones of the Englishman show wider melodic curves than those of the American, and also more rapid changes." So Miss Leigh and Mr. Howard were sentenced to listen to my voice for at least an hour each day, and to imitate the cadence and rhythm of the Georgia speech. By the time shooting began most of the British staccato was gone from the tongues of both of them and it was not long before they had changed "bean" into "been," given up the broad *a* for the sake of the Confederacy and acquired the Southern habit of dropping the voice at the end of most sentences.

I think Vivien's greatest trouble was with the words "love" and "mother."

"Make it rhyme with the way I say 'of,' " I told her.

"Oh," she said, her blue eyes growing rounder and larger until they seemed to fill the whole of her lovely face, "Oh! You pronounce your *o* like *au*. I've got it now."

She did have it, too. "Muther" and "luve" the words became, and there was no more trouble with them.

Neither did she have difficulty with such words as "talk" and "walk," which your Southerner pronounces "tawk" and "wawk," and only a suggestion was needed to change her "coffee" into Confederate "cawfee."

Leslie Howard, putting on his gray uniform, put on, too, his Southern accent, spoke of "gu-ils" instead of "gels,' pronounced the state where the Shenandoah Valley campaign was fought "Virginya" instead of "Virginia," and loosened his jaw to get the round, full *o* of the Southern "hope" and "corps."

That *o* sound gave Mr. Howard more trouble than any other. Once, even, he asked me if I couldn't persuade the script writer to change a line:

"It's so full of those beastly *o*'s of yours," he said. "Listen: 'Don't go tweaking his nose any more.' Couldn't you get rid of a few *o*'s for me?"

"No, Professor Higgins," I told him, "you'll just have to go on trying. Maybe you'll get good enough to play in Pygmalion!"

I believe David O. Selznick was happy about the slight compromise we made on Southern accent, but from time to time he would approach me with a worried expression, usually just after he had seen the daily rushes.

"Do you think the audience will understand a single word Mammy says?" he asked, running his hands through his thick, curly hair until it stood straight on end. "Come in here and listen."

I followed him into the projection room and watched while Melanie and Mammy ascended the stairs at the Rhett Butler house in Atlanta—the house that Rhett built with turrets and doodads and fancy scrollwork and bad taste to please Scarlett, who wanted to outshine all the newly rich in Atlanta and make her old friends green with envy.

Mammy wept, dried her eyes on her apron and told Melanie how "Mistuh Rhett done los' his mi' since Bonnie was killed trying to make her pony take a high jump.

"Den dis evenin' Miss Scarlett holler th'u de do' dat de fune'l set fer termorrer mawnin' and he says, 'Try dat an' ah kills yer termorrer. Does you think ah'm gwine put mah chile in de dahk when she so skeered uv it?' Yesum, it's de gawd's truf. He ain't gwine let us bury dat chile."

"Can't we tone Mammy down a little?" Selznick urged. But he capitulated when I reminded him we had to be consistent and Mammy had been talking like a plantation darkey from the beginning. Matter of fact, he always capitulated about the Negroes' accent, and the colored persons in the movie sound as if they had stepped from the Uncle Remus books.

Hattie McDaniel, born in Tennessee, and Oscar Polk, born in Arkansas, play the roles of Mammy and Pork. They found the dialect easy but it had to be taught to Butterfly McQueen, who had lived most of her life in Harlem. But, as Prissy, Butterfly turns in a fine performance with a remarkable old plantation darkey dialect.

The script writer followed the dialogue of the novel faithfully and when it was necessary to write additional lines Mr. Selznick sent for me.

"I want an exclamation for Pork in this scene," he said once. "What would he say? Would 'Holy Moses' be all right?"

"His natural remark under these circumstances would be 'Gre't Gawd a'mighty!" I answered. "But the board of censorship won't stand for that. Let's have him say 'Gre't Jehoshaphat.' "

That exclamation, so familiar to Georgians who know plantation Negroes, aroused much comment on the Selznick lot, but that was nothing to the furor that rose when I said the Negroes at the station in Atlanta would not say "Merry Christmas" but "Chris'mus Give" or "Chris'mus gif'."

During slavery time, I explained, the Negroes always came up to the Big House on Christmas morning, dressed in their Sunday clothes and expecting gifts which the Master and Mistis always provided. As the plantation owner and his wife came out on the piazza to speak to the slaves, the blacks called their greetings, the women and children making sweeping curtsies and the men removing their hats to bow low:

"Mawin' Mistis! Mawin' Mawstah! Chris'mus Give," they would call, grinning with pleasure at the thought of the dram from Mawstah and the presents Mistis would provide.

So the phrase Merry Christmas was out and the Negroes called "Chris'mus Gif'" and for days afterward Director Victor Fleming greeted me on the set not with "Good morning" but with "Chris'mus Gif'."

Well, the picture is finished now; the editors have done their work. Perhaps I shall become a woman without a country; not allowed to live in the South and refused entrance into the Nawth, shuttling back and forth for the rest of my days between Yankeedom and Dixie Land because nobody likes the Southern accent in *Gone With the Wind.*

———————————

Collier's, December 16, 1939

LOST COLUMNS FROM HOLLYWOOD

When Richard Harwell collected Sue's 1939 news columns written in Hollywood and published in the *Macon Telegraph*, he somehow missed four of them. John Wiley, Jr., author of the *Scarlett Letter* and co-author of *Margaret Mitchell's* Gone With the Wind: *A Bestseller's Odyssey from Atlanta to Hollywood*, had copies of the articles and informed Harwell of their existence, but the book was too far along in publication for the articles to be included in *White Columns in Hollywood*.

John has graciously provided copies of these articles for this book.

Miss Myrick Becomes Fannie Squeers Again and Is Shocked

Accustomed as I am to driving the Chevy from the Fredonia down to the garage and walking only a block to work, it seems very metropolitan to me now to be riding an inter-urban trolley to work each day, reading the paper as I ride and trying to feel like the big business woman.

Tonight, urban-transiting to Santa Monica from the Selznick International Pictures (hereinafter referred to as SIP), I sat beside a man who was reading the *New Testament* which had the words of Christ in red letters, and across from me sat a couple about high school age who were necking pretty strenuously. She was a thin little thing who looked as if she had never had a square meal and she snuggled her elaborately curled little head down on the broad shoulders of the boy and (honest, I'm telling the truth) I looked away in embarrassment at the look on the big boy's face and dropped my eyes on the red-lettered Bible verse that said:

"Love thy neighbor as thyself."

And I thought, "What a fine situation for Fannie Squeers!" (Fannie Squeers was the pen name Sue used for her advice column in the Macon Telegraph.)

But it's a long way from Fannie and her advice to SIP, and things are still happening out here with the rapidity of machine gun fire.

Rat-tat-tat! First thing this morning I had a conference with Walter Plunkett, who is head of the wardrobe department and who has designed the most ravishing clothes for Scarlett O'Hara. We looked at old photographs and talked about funny head dresses and exclaimed over the way moustaches and beards looked in the Sixties and agreed about how hoop skirts for elderly ladies made them look so enormous about the hips.

And right in the midst of our talk, in came a handsome young man, dressed just as you expect a movie actor to be dressed in his casual moments. He wore dark brown pants with leather braces (nobody who looked so elegant could wear suspenders—they have to be braces) that looked like the Duke of Windsor might have worn when he was being casual with Wallis. And his shirt of a deep, dark green was open at the neck and he was tie-less, but he wore a luscious scarf of dark brown and green knotted carelessly about his manly throat. And the coat— well the coat was what the well-dressed young man wears for a weekend in the country, a la *Esquire*. It was a plaid of brown and tan, loose and patch-pockety and worn with that air which manages to let you know there are braces underneath so the pleated-top trousers set off the best possible effect for the wedge shape of a broad-shouldered, slender-waisted young gentleman.

Well, "Handsome Harry" was there for coaching on Southern accent until Will Price came in and said I was to go to talk Southern a while to Miss Vivien Leigh (pronounced the same as in General Robert E. Lee) who, you know by this time, is to play Scarlett O'Hara.

Miss Leigh is very beautiful, very gracious and utterly charming. She wore dark green slacks and a soft shirt to match, and her magnolia-petal skin glowed against the color. Her dusky hair curled softly about her shoulders and she looked so beautiful it was hard for me to keep my mind on her accent.

Delmar Warren and the others in Macon who love pretty rooms would have had fits over the charming room in which we sat.

The living room was bright with the California sunshine that filtered in through the Venetian blinds at a window at least eight feet wide and reaching from floor to ceiling. That window was near the corner of the eastern side of the rectangular room and was not far from the fireplace which was framed in a mirror reaching from hearth to ceiling—a mirror about 12 feet wide that reflected the opposite side of the room where French doors opened on a terrace and showed a glimpse of the purple blossoms of the bougainvillea.

A recessed corner balanced the window space on the other side of the fireplace and in it was a love seat in green, black and yellow pattern that beautifully set off the taupe color of drapes and sofa and two large easy chairs. The rug was a shade darker taupe. There were two dignified, tall, slender chairs done in the same shade of green as that on the love seat and there were two more chairs in yellow.

Swedish modern tables and bookracks stood in just the right places. They were natural finished gum or some other light-colored wood and all about were bowls and vases of flowers.

Near the entrance was a huge vase of calla lilies (the silly things grow wild around here, it appears), and in low bowls about the room were varicolored garden flowers whose names I don't know.

It drives me wild, anyhow, that I do not recognize many trees or flowers in California. I need Hebe Casson to tell me names of these foreign shrubs and trees and flowers. I have found out that the lacy-foliaged tree that grows in such profusion here is a pepper tree but whether it grows cayenne or black pepper nobody can tell me.

Matter of fact, I don't even know whether it is the morning pepper or the evening pepper!

("Get back to the studio," I can hear you muttering.)

So—back I go. I skipped my lunch hour to see some shots of an old film because George Cukor wanted me to see some Negro actors who are possibilities for *Gone With the Wind* and I had a sandwich and a glass of milk while I watched, along with Will Price, who is a dialogue coach at SIP.

Then back to the office to read some inter-office communications. (You can always be sure there will be one or more of these on your desk when you return after an absence, no matter how brief. Some days, I'm going to lie in wait for the boy and catch him putting the envelope on my desk. Up to now I have had a feeling it is done by Rumpelstiltskin, or maybe it's the Seven Dwarfs.)

I dictated some inter-office communications of my own. (And how strange it seems to dictate after I have thought with the typewriter keys under my fingers for so long!) Then I went to the property department to talk with Eddie Boyle, who is a delightful person and a most efficient interior decorator.

You'll love the furniture he has acquired for Tara and for the home of Aunt Pittypat, and when you see GWTW (as of course you will) plan to see it twice. The first time you can look at the show, the second time you can watch for the interesting sets. Mr. Boyle is going to make it all look so much like the old Georgia furniture you are accustomed to it would make you homesick if you saw the movie in a foreign land.

It is downright staggering to me to discover the million things that have to be done to make a picture as it should be made.

Take, for instance, the well that is to be in the backyard at Tara. Wilbur Kurtz drew a picture of the way country wells look—not a city well of brick and round in shape and citified-looking. Just a square-boxed well with a windlass that creaks and with shingles of uneven size and that look of having stood for years. And Wilbur even drew a picture of the gourd from which the darkies drink.

Now the well is all finished and standing out at Tara on "Forty Acres" and I almost tried to draw myself a bucket of water from it.

Mr. Boyle took me in the "Mill" where expert craftsman turn lumber into finished products of whatever design may be desired. The place is almost as big as Willingham Sash and Door works.

So, after pushing back my eyes, which were sticking out two inches in front of my face, I went back again to the Melanie room and read another inter-off ... . Yeah, you guessed it. And so, home to Santa Monica.

Macon Telegraph, January 21, 1939

Hold your Hats, Girls: Myrick Tells of Seeing Gable

Rally 'round, girls! Gentlemen, you may as well stop reading right here.

Today I met Clark Gable.

Director George Cukor's secretary telephoned me to bring all the pictures I had that would show types of neckwear for gentlemen of the sixties and come to his office to discuss costume design and wardrobe for Selznick International Pictures.

Hastily running the comb through my hair, applying a bit of lipstick and brushing some of the shine off my nose, I laid down my glasses (remembering Dorothy Parker's crack about girls who wear them) and walked sedately to Mr. Cukor's office.

There, on a sofa beside Mr. Cukor, sat the idol of America's feminine heart, the man who is to play Rhett Butler in *Gone With the Wind.*

He wore a creamy-yellow shirt that looked silken, a four-in-hand of bright yellow and raspberry stripe, a tannish-taupe-colored coat and gray trousers and he looked very fresh and just-out-of-the-band-boxish.

He rose as I entered and as Mr. Cukor said, 'May I, etc." And I started to mutter, "How-dy do," but Mr. Gable stepped forward two steps and with the utmost cordiality offered his hand and said he was delighted to meet me.

He couldn't have been more deferential if I'd been—well—say, the wife of a vice president.

So we sat down, at Mr. Cukor's invitation, on the sofa. And all of you who want to get a thrill out of this, go ahead. I sat right beside Mr. Gable and showed him neckties and collars of the War Between the States era.

The costume designer, Walter Plunkett, had 10 sketches to show Mr. Gable; for as you right well know, Rhett Butler is a dashing young man and in the *Gone With the Wind* production he will have many changes of clothes and look very handsome and debonair.

There was much talk of fancy vests and shirts with little ruffles down the front and there was much showing of fabrics and discussion of boots and hats.

Then the conference was over and I returned to the hum-drum office job, writing out what I think about booths at the bazaar in Atlanta in 1862 and making notes on suggestions for Southern touches for the barbecue at Twelve Oaks and so on.

But early this morning a trip to the make-up department was exciting and fascinating. The make-up man was trying out various shades on the lovely face of Miss Vivien Leigh—and make no mistake she is a beautiful girl. Even with her soft dark hair pulled back, like beauty operators will fix it to keep the make-up away from the hair, she looked sweet enough to win the heart of anybody.

On the large dressing table before her were at least 50 brushes, 20 jars and large bottles and scores of little tiny bottles and tubes and boxes of this and that. There was enough make-up to last Macon's Little Theatre for, roughly estimating, about 10 years!

And that was just one table. There were four or five more scattered in various little rooms where other girls and men were getting tryouts for make-up. You see, the eye of the Technicolor camera is hard to satisfy and the make-up man tries many different styles and has the photographer see what is best.

These are submitted to Producer David O Selznick and Mr. Cukor for final approval and then things are ready to go.

The gentleman who is to take the role of Jonas Wilkerson (Robert Gleckler) was being kidded about looking too much like a gentleman for playing an overseer and somebody kept telling him he had no right to look like one and the make-up man put on more whiskers and took off the moustache and then took off the beard and put on the moustache and the laughter and the good-natured raillery went on.

Charles Hamilton and the Tarleton twins were getting sideburns attached and trimmed and Suellen and Carreen were trying various hairdos. And it was all very exciting and strange to the newcomer to the set.

I went out to Tara again today and it grows more and more like the Clayton County home of the O'Haras. And the trees and shrubs are progressing fine. Tomorrow, the Bermuda grass is to be put on the yard and the boxwood set out and I am to confer with Miss Florence Yoch and the art department again about yellow jassamine and wisteria and the cedars to plant in the family burial grounds.

Sunday afternoon I went riding and visited the Pasadena Playhouse which turned me green with envy. It is six stories high and has dressing rooms, wardrobe rooms, small production and rehearsal room, gymnasium, roof garden and everything else a theatrical group would want.

Sunday Macon Telegraph and News, January 22, 1939

Miss Myrick Amazed at Work Before Shooting

Never again shall I be able to look at a moving picture with only enjoyment of the story that unfolds before me! I'll be thinking about all the million things the producer and his corps of assistants had to do to get ready for the shooting.

As you probably know, *Gone With the Wind* is to be in Technicolor. Well, yesterday, Eric Stacey, assistant to George Cukor, shot Technicolor tests to see how costumes, upholstery, furniture, fabrics and earth looked to the camera.

A call sheet noted that a truck should be ready to pick up things at 8 o'clock, that the stand-ins should be at the make-up room at 7:30 and that the art, wardrobe and property departments should have everything ready, "as discussed."

The strangest thing of all to my mind is the fact that the soil is to be sprayed to become the shade of orange-red that Georgia dirt is. California soil is a sort of sand-color or with some darker, richer dirt mixed in it, and in order to have the fields about Tara look as they did in Clayton County, Georgia, the field has been sprayed with red paint.

This color had to be tested and the director also wanted to see what effect was produced by the blue curtains, the floral design in the carpets, the gay and bright colors of the costumes and how a white dress showed up against certain backgrounds and so on.

Out at Forty Acres, the cameramen began shooting at 9 o'clock in the usual bright California sunshine. And about 40 minutes later, in rolled a fog as thick as the ones that shroud San Francisco or London!

It was, perhaps, the tail-end of the snow storm that the papers tell us blanketed the East.

Yesterday was the first chilly day I've seen since I arrived. A spring suit felt warm enough every day until Saturday, but when the fog came in I wanted a fur coat.

Only I didn't stay out long; for I had to go to work on accent with Leslie Howard and Miss Vivien Leigh, who will take the roles of Ashley Wilkes and Scarlett O'Hara, respectively.

The initial explanation of the differences between Southern-American accent and the accent of the Britisher were explained by Will Price, a dialogue coach for the picture.

Some of the Little Theatre directors at Macon will remember Mr. Price. Three years ago he was with the Federal Theater in Atlanta and he came down to see one of the shows produced at Macon when Fred Killian was director of the Little Theatre. He met a number of Maconites at a party which Mrs. Piercy Chestney gave at the "Dug-Out" and still talks enthusiastically about Piercy and his hobby and Mrs. Chestney and the delightful party she gave.

Mr. Price explained to Mr. Howard that Southerners speak with more open vowels and that they have a richer rounder fuller sort of speech, and Mr. Howard listened attentively and showed complete understanding by his comments. He has lived in the United States long enough to know the vast differences between speech in Ohio and in Texas, for instance, and he realizes that the speech of the New Yorker is different from that of the Bostonian, but he has never realized what the Southern speech is like until now.

Poor man! He was greatly bewildered by the way I talked. When Mr. Price left me to talk with Mr. Howard for a while, he had to ask me to repeat about half of what I said.

George Cukor wants the actors to listen to me talk for he thinks my accent is very thick Southern and the actors will absorb just enough of it to sound right over the mike.

Mr. Cukor says I wouldn't believe my own voice if I heard it recorded and he thinks that every Southerner would scream and run out of the movie house if they heard an accent like mine in *Gone With the Wind*.

He is an astute director I believe, for he wants the accent to be only slightly suggestive of a Southerner and he is doing everything to avoid what he calls a "phony accent." And his ear is remarkably keen, too. He recognizes the differences between poor-white Southern and Negro Southern and the speech of an educated Southerner; and that is more than many persons can do even when they've been born in the South.

So, with me, it is not a question of "Listen, the Wind!" But a matter of Listen, *Gone With the Wind*!

Macon Telegraph, January 23, 1939

Shooting Stars and Miss Myrick
Gives Clark Gable an A-Plus

The official flag of the Confederate States of America flies over the studios of Selznick International Pictures, for the shooting of *Gone With the Wind* has begun. Bees buzzing around on the first honey-gathering day of spring are lazybones compared with the production department of SIP. The evening before the first camera began to turn, I left the studios at 7:30 and I left early!

From the time I took off my hat at 9:10 a.m., until I left, I rushed from this place to that and back again. To start the morning off, I scooted down to Stage 14 to look at a horse for Rhett Butler to ride. The day before, we had selected horses for the Tarleton twins and a handsome white horse for Gerald O'Hara. And if any girls in Bibb County envy my association with Clark Gable, that will probably be nothing compared to the youngsters who learn now that I saw Hi-Ho, Silver's horse doing tricks. He followed his trainer upstairs, without being led, and he reared and pawed and did whatever he was told. Hi-Ho is the horse Gerald will ride.

But the magnificent mount for Rhett was selected today because of his ability to do a perfect single foot, lifting his forefeet high and performing like the show horse he is.

Rushing back to my office I encountered the prop man who had been looking for me, and we decided about the boxes the O'Hara girls used to take their evening dresses to the barbecue, we selected the sort of wedding ring and engagement ring Scarlett would wear, and discussed the kind of plants that would grow in pots in Aunt Pitty's house.

Before I got back to the office this time, I met George Cukor, who wanted me on Stage 12 to discuss some plans for the bazaar and to go to Stage 3 to decide some things about Mammy at Tara.

Back we went to Mr. Cukor's office, where he held a conference with Monty Westmore and Walter Plunkett on hairdressers and we looked at some daguerreotypes and some pictures I had brought out with me (thanks to Mrs. Ben Smith and Telamon Cuyler and some other friends) and finally decided to look once more at some screen tests of hairdressings tried several days before.

Mr. Plunkett, costume designer, and Mr. Westmore, head of make-up, and I saw the takes and they went one way and I another.

Without stopping to breathe, I went to consult with Joe Platt, who has come here from New York to dress the sets for the production. Mr. Platt and I discussed what sort of flowers might be in the parlor at Tara, how there should be steps for Ellen's bedside, what to do about hassocks, whether there were too many pictures on the wall and a score of other details.

Then lunch!

The lunch room on the lot is a fine place. The food is pleasing and there are always some interesting persons with whom you may eat. It is not so much fun as I had in Macon lunching with Bob Quinlan, Perry Mahone, Ed Ferguson and Elliott Dunwody, but it's nice. Today, I ate with Annie Laurie Kurtz (Mrs. Wilbur), who is out here helping her husband on historical details. And we spent the lunch hour talking about things back in Georgia. Of course, Mrs. Kurtz loves Macon, for her daughter, Annie Laurie, is at Wesleyan on a UDC scholarship.

But there wasn't much time for lunch today. Mrs. Wilbur Kurtz had to talk to Laura Hope Crews, who is Aunt Pitty, because Will Price and George Cukor and I thought Mrs. Kurtz's lady-like voice would be excellent for Aunt Pitty to pattern after.

I hurried back to the office for a conference with a writer on some dialogue for the script, and before we'd finished, Mr. Cukor called me to listen to a rehearsal. Miss Vivien Leigh and Clark Gable were going over a scene and Mr. Cukor wanted me to say whether their accent sounded phony or just right.

The way Miss Leigh said "war" sounds jut as it does when Mrs. W. D. Lamar or Mrs. Piercy Chestney or Mrs. Fran Jones or any other educated UDC lady said it, and I pronounced her perfect and suggested David O. Selznick give her an A-Plus on the lesson.

Mr. Gable got a similar rating.

Then we all went over to projection room six to see some rushes of scenes shot a few days before.

On the screen was a picture of Miss Barbara O'Neil, as Ellen O'Hara. She looked very dignified and sweet with her hair done in the typical Southern 1860 fashion. Mr. Cukor said, "Sue, how do you like that hairstyle?"

"I am just crazy about it," I replied emphatically.

"Well, I do think you might show some enthusiasm," chuckled Mr. Selznick.

There was general laughter in the projection room, and I was happy for the darkness that hid my blushes. But I couldn't hide my enthusiasm over Olivia de Havilland, in the costume designed for Melanie. Forgetting the little by-play over Ellen's hair arrangement, I said I thought Melanie was the loveliest thing I ever saw, and the whole company shouted with laughter.

There was discussion of Mr. Gable's taking some lessons on the waltz and there was much kidding about how well he could dance, and he said he didn't need any lesson on waltzing.

"There is nothing to making a waltz look old-fashioned except to hold the girl far away from you, is there, Miss Myrick?" He appealed to me.

Then he stood up and holding his arms as if he were holding a partner in the waltz, he said, "Like this—just about the same, only not close to her, isn't it?"

"Not so close and not so much fun," I said.

"And not so much fun," he agreed, showing the dimple and the white teeth in his famous smile.

Back, then, to Mr. Cukor's office to select some Negroes for roles in the cast. We picked a cook, an assistant to the cook, some housemaids, a coachman for Ellen's carriage, some little boys to do various things about the house and two men servants. And I can't wait for you to see the little Negro boy who is to perform the task Margaret Mitchell described in the book—shooing the chickens off the O'Hara lawn.

The colored members of the cast were sent to wardrobe and while they were being costumed, Mr. Cukor and I went to Miss Leigh's bungalow dressing room, where Mr. Selznick wanted us to see Miss Leigh's costumes.

We sat on easy chairs in the living room, and Miss Leigh paraded beautiful gowns, billowing in soft folds over hoop skirts and ruffled petticoats. The style of the Sixties enhances the natural beauty of the actress and the costumer had done a marvelous piece of work. I'm afraid you'll have to sit through the picture twice so you can realize just how perfect in detail the gowns are.

Me—I'm never going to be able to just sit and enjoy a picture as the story unfolds. I'll be watching for the things I know somebody has figured on and worked out.

Macon Telegraph, January 30, 1939

LESLIE HOWARD

HE sits in sun on patio in shorts, locket about his neck, red hair glinting in sun, lounging in chair, talking to coach.

SHE calls from window above—wears filmy pajamas, robe carelessly, not much thrown over the pajamas.

"Darling, may I interrupt? What time are you going to the dentist today?"

"I don't know. They cancelled my call at studio for stills and disrupted my entire day so I don't know."

"Shall I make an appointment for you?"

"Yes, darling, if you will."

"What time shall I make it?"

"It doesn't matter—anytime you can get it for me."

Ten minutes later. She opens window again, leaning way out, blonded hair with permanent ends disarranged—not so good to look at but what I can believe is that Lambert was right when he said, "A good lay."

"Darling, excoose me, may I interrupt again?"

"Certainly, dear. What is it?"

"You have an appointment for four-thirty with the dentist. Is that all right? Or shall I change it for you?"

"Why, no, dear, that's all right if it's all right with you?"

"Well, I thought you might drop me off at Bedford's to get my hair done at four-thirty. Then we could go together."

"Of course, dear, I'll be glad to drop you off there."

"But if you have an appointment for four-thirty and I have, also, how can we get there together?"

"Well, dear, I can drop you off a few minutes early and then go on to my appointment, cawnt I?'

"Well, yes, darling, I suppose so."

She starts to go away. He calls:

"Dear, why not let the hair dresser come here?"

"Oh, I think not, darlin'. It would be so complicated. Let's go there."

"All right, at four-thirty."

Five minutes later: SHE: "Excoose me again, darlin', but don't you want to get a hair cut?"

He, running hands through hair lazily, rubbing hands over face as if the effort to decide about hair cut is VERY difficult.

"Well, yes, dear, I suppose it would be better to get it trimmed a bit."

"Well, how would you like to let's both go to Westmore's."

"Oh no, he's terrible. We don't want to go there."

"Oh no, he isn't. He is good. Isn't he the man who cut your hair at Metro's?"

"I don't know, darling. Do you want to go to him?"

"Well, I thought I might get a manicure while you got a hair cut and we could go together a little before four-thirty."

"Are you going to let him do your hair, too?"

"Oh, no! He cawnt do hair. He's terrible. I could get a manicure, though."

"Well, what would you do about your hair?"

"I don't know. I have an appointment at four-thirty at Madame Westley's."

"Oh, you have?"

"Yes, darling, I just told you."

"Did you?"

"Yes, when I first awsked you about going to the dentist's."

"Oh, well this is growing complicated. What shall we do? Cawnt you have him come here to do your manicure?"

"Well, no-o-o. It's no good getting a manicure here. It's so complicated. And it costs a lot more. (This with the look of "aren't I a sweet little thing to save money for you that way?")

"Well, darling, it is very complicated isn't it? What shall we do?"

"I don't know, dear. What do you want to do? Do you really want a hair cut?"

"Well, I don't know. It's all so complicated. I might get a bit of a trim."

"Well, darling, what do you think we'd better do?" (Looking a little injured and somewhat like a martyr.) "Would you rather just go on to the dentist and let me go on to the hair dresser's?"

"Certainly not, darling." (Being emphatic.) "No, indeed. Look here, I'll tell you. Why can't you get an appointment for me at your hair dresser's and I can let him just trim my hair while you get yours done?"

"Oh, no, that would not do at all."

"Why not?"

"Oh, she cawnt cut your hair. And besides she has appointments all awfternoon. She couldn't get you in. And she cawnt give me a manicure."

"Oh dear! This IS complicated, isn't it? What shall we do? Maybe we can skip the manicure. I tell you what, dear; I'll give you a manicure. How would you like that?"

"Well, I don't know, darling. Maybe we could just let you drop me at Westmore's as you go to the dentist and I could get the manicure then."

"And what about your hair, dear?"

"Oh, I couldn't let Westmore do my hair."

"Oh, dear whatever shall we do? This is all so complicated."

"There's the telephone, dear. I'll come back."

Returns later.

"Scoose me, darling, again, please, for interrupting. That was Marlene and she says we are expected to lunch at her house at two so that settles it all very nicely. I'll just cancel your appointment with the dentist and we can get me a manicure after we leave Marlene's."

Unpublished Manuscript, 1939

DAVID O. SELZNICK, THE UNPREDICTABLE

He Has Given His Best to *Gone With the Wind*

At the age of 20, David O. Selznick began a career that was to lead to his supreme achievement, the production of *Gone With the Wind*, the motion picture of Margaret Mitchell's novel of the South and the War Between the States. It was in 1922 that the youthful Selznick made his first picture, a "quickie" of Luis Angel Firpo training for his fight with Dempsey—a picture that cost about $500 and brought the maker $3500.

That success started the young man's career, for he had long been interested in motion pictures because of his father, Lewis J. Selznick, who was a pioneer maker and distributor of films. Through successive steps, the young man climbed until he came to head his own company, Selznick International Pictures with studios at Culver City, California, in 1935. A little more than a year later he bought the motion picture rights to *Gone With the Wind* for $50,000.

Working in what is regarded in Hollywood as a "tiny studio," without the facilities of a great producing office, David O. Selznick has created the most extensive and elaborate motion picture of all time. It is a product almost wholly of his own efforts and every step of the making of the picture was strictly under his guidance.

There was plenty to supervise, you may be sure. Making that picture required one million man-hours of labor and the cost was around four million dollars. It took three-and-a-half years to make it, too.

Often, as I watched the work about the studio and down on the back lot, which we knew as "Forty Acres," I would shake my head and say to myself:

"If we'd had as many men in the Confederate Army as they have working on this picture, I bet we would have licked those Yankees!"

Hardly a foot of film was shot without the careful attention of Producer Selznick. Scarcely a nail was driven in a set, or a stitch sewed into a costume, or a camera threaded with its three strips of film that Selznick did not supervise it.

It is one of Selznick's many innovations that Technicolor is employed as it is in the making of *Gone With the Wind*. He has broken many precedents in Hollywood and advanced many new ideas but none have intrigued him more than the use of Technicolor. Among the first to use this successful adaptation of color photography to the making of motion pictures, he has made another advance in the art in making *Gone With the Wind*.

For he believes that the story should not be subjected to the medium—that the producer should never rely on color instead of the story to stimulate interest. So, in making the longest picture ever made, Selznick has used Technicolor to enhance the presentation of Margaret Mitchell's absorbing story of Scarlett O'Hara.

There is another thing which Selznick has done in making *Gone With the Wind* that is unprecedented. There is a scene showing the thousands of wounded Confederates outside the railroad station in Atlanta, with nurses and doctors working among them. This shot will bring an ache to your heart and a great choking in your throat, for it will tell you that The Cause is lost—the Confederacy has failed.

There is drama and heart-ache in that shot as in no other scene I have witnessed on any screen. Of course Margaret Mitchell thought out the scene but it remained for Selznick to visualize it.

Technically, there never was a shot like it. The largest camera boom ever used in a motion picture was contrived for this shot through leasing a contractor's huge crane. It was 85 feet long and weighed 120 tons.

To my mind the most interesting thing about the shot is the fact that it was conceived and laid out by David O. Selznick more that two years in advance of the time it was executed.

For David Selznick is an amazing person. He not only planned big boom shots of such magnitude as nobody ever dared before, but he directed the color of Scarlett's frocks to bring out the best in her as well as the best effect in Technicolor; he saw over and over again every foot of the 475,000 feet of film exposed; he spent hours over the preparation of the script; he interviewed personally hundreds of candidates for roles in the picture; he kept fingers on everything concerned with the production.

Myriads of details needed attention. Construction required a million board feet of lumber and five tons of hardware. He used 1000 horses, 375 assorted animals and 450 assorted vehicles. The Atlanta fire scene was one of the largest conflagrations ever made for a film. The set showing the city of Atlanta as it was in the Sixties was the largest ever built. It contained 53 buildings and 7,000 feet of streets. Peachtree Street alone was 3000 feet long.

No wonder that Selznick, who has always done the unpredictable thing in his professional life with great success, counts this latest achievement, *Gone With the Wind*, the hardest task and the one productive of most joy to him.

If published, no publication information available. About 1940

TIME MUST SERVE

or

You Don't Chop Cotton in April

People around the Selznick International Pictures lot in Culver City, California, spoke of my office as the Melanie Room because they considered it quiet and unpretentious, but the huge room, the leather lounge chairs, the oversized mahogany desk gave me a feeling of insignificance that added to the gloom which enveloped me. As technical adviser for the movie *Gone With the Wind*, I was discovering that living for many years in Georgia had failed to give me much of the information that producers, directors, property men, costumers, and actors had expected me to provide.

On the majestic desk before me lay the latest inter-office communication, dictated by Producer David O. Selznick, and laid there a short while ago by a sixth assistant to the assistant to the secretary to the producer. It read:

TO: Miss Myrick
DATE: Jan 15, 1939
FROM: DOS
SUBJECT: GWTW
Dear Miss Myrick:
Please arrange with Transportation to see the location on which we propose to shoot the scenes that show Gerald O'Hara riding over his plantation the evening before the barbecue. Report to me whether you think the field is suitable for the cotton chopping scene.

I looked at the fernlike pattern on the carpet, where the California sunlight shadowed the pepper tree foliage, and I wished I had never seen a pepper tree or a eucalyptus tree or the inside of a movie studio. For I was deeply concerned about my task as adviser on Southern manners and customs and accent for the movie version of Margaret

Mitchell's best-seller. I knew that countless Southerners regarded the book as a perfect picture of the South of the sixties and the Reconstruction era. I knew that the million readers of this book stood waiting with chips on shoulders, virtually daring the movie version to fail in any particular. I hated the thought of Fort Sumter's being fired on again and I didn't like to think of Georgia's seceding again from the Union. And I was scared.

That inter-office communication had me upset. I knew that Gerald O'Hara's ride preceded the barbecue scene by one day and that the barbecue was to announce President Lincoln's call for volunteers as well as Melanie Hamilton's engagement to Ashley Wilkes. That meant the date of the scene was set for mid-April, and mid-April is not the time for cotton chopping in North Georgia.

I shook off my gloom, congratulated myself upon knowing when cotton is chopped, telephoned a secretary and dictated an inter-office communication of my own:

TO: DOS
DATE: January 15, 1939
SUBJECT: GWTW
Dear Mr. Selznick:
I shall be glad to look at the field for cotton chopping, as you requested. But I wished to call attention to the fact that April 15 is too early for cotton chopping in North Georgia. The scene might better show the Negroes plowing the fields for planting.

When I telephoned Transportation, next morning, about the trip to location, I was informed that Mr. Selznick had cancelled the trip and I was relieved, thinking in my naïve fashion that the cotton chopping scene was out and I could devote my attention to other details. There were many.

The third assistant property man wanted me to select the right sort of wedding ring for Scarlett O'Hara; the assistant script writer wanted me to draw a floor plan of the house where Melanie lived in Atlanta; the set dresser wanted to know if rag rugs were right for Aunt Pittypat's bedroom and would I look at the furniture he had selected for her parlor and how about those wax flowers under glass for the mantel? The wardrobe director, the costume designer, the director and the producer wanted me to see Vivien Leigh try on her green sprigged muslin for the barbecue scene, to decide just how low-necked it could be.

Director George Cukor wanted me to accompany the woman who

was planning the landscaping of the grounds about Tara to tell her what sort of trees grew there and what a scuppernong arbor looked like.

Somebody wanted me to see the cemetery where the little O'Haras were buried and tell them what headstones in Southern cemeteries were like. The first assistant director wanted me to decide what kind of wreath should be on the front door at the Rhett Butler home in Atlanta when Bonnie was dead. Cukor wanted to know what would happen at family prayers and did they sing hymns at prayer time?

And in-between, I listened to accents of various persons, most of whom were listed as Southern born—South Dakota or Southern California, that is.

So, busy with one thing and another, I forgot about chopping cotton in mid-April until I received a second communication on the subject:

FROM: DOS
DATE: Feb. 12, 1939
TO: Myrick
SUBJECT: GWTW
Dear Miss Myrick:
Please arrange with Transportation to see the location on which we propose...

Except for the date, the message was identical with the one I had received almost a month before. Again I telephoned for a stenographer and again I dictated a memo:

You may recall that I wrote you on Jan. 15 about the cotton chopping scene. The script shows plainly that O'Hara's ride is the afternoon before the barbecue; the date of the barbecue is fixed by reason of the announcement of Mr. Lincoln's call for volunteers. Since that date is approximately mid-April, I must remind you that it is not cotton chopping time; the cotton seeds have not even been planted by mid-April.

May I suggest that the scene be changed to plowing the fields?

The reply to that memo was a telephone call from Mr. Selznick's secretary, who asked that I come to the producer's office for a conference.

"We've got to have that cotton chopping scene" was the gist of Selznick's argument; he had engaged the Hall Johnson choir at several thousand dollars a day to sing while they chopped. The scene had to be in.

My theme song was "You don't chop cotton in mid-April in North Georgia." I repeated the statement I had put into the inter-office communication and suggested, once more, that the Negroes plow instead of chop.

The producer finally said he would consider the matter of using the Hall Johnson choir in another scene, and once more, I considered the cotton chopping episode closed. I could take up my argument with Art Director Bill Menzies on the subject of Spanish moss in the trees around Tara.

"If you'll let me have Spanish moss in this scene, I'll give a couple of inches to you off the size of Twelve Oaks," he pleaded. For we had been fighting for days on the subject of the size of Twelve Oaks, home of the John Wilkes family. The original plans called for a house the size and proportions of the Palace at Versailles and the gardens would have dwarfed those at Mount Vernon.

I was heady because I had won in the altercation over the size and plans for Tara and thought I would take the victory in the Battle of Twelve Oaks. The director had reluctantly let down the scale of grandeur at Tara to conform to the author's description of the O'Hara home in Clayton County: "a clumsy, sprawling building that crowned the rise of ground."

Not that I didn't get criticized for it! Every time we shot a scene at Scarlett's bedroom or in the dining room or the parlor at Tara, everybody—the director, producer, cameraman—scowled at me and muttered that the place was entirely too small.

But I was ready to go to the mat about Twelve Oaks. I was willing to have the home indicate the Wilkes family was a wealthy and aristocratic one, that they had come from Virginia to the newest colony, and that their house would be architecturally superior.

Still, I could not accept the prospectus without a struggle. The drawings showed a front porch with two-story columns of about the size and number of those which flank the entrance of the Pennsylvania Station in New York City. The hallway was big enough to house a whole building of the average Georgia home. The stairway had a double approach, a curve as wide as that on a half-mile race track and more steps than the Washington Monument.

There were some thirty water color sketches of the house and I groaned when I looked at them:

"You can't do this to me! You CAN'T!"

Art Director Menzies laughed. "It's only a hovel but we call it home."

Then he explained that he had reduced the size and elegance of Tara and he had to have one house which would please the people who would go to the movie, GWTW. The picture had been bally-hooed for more than two years, the script had been written and rewritten by the top writers of the nation; the country had been toured to find an "unknown" to play Scarlett; thousands of people had written to Selznick, giving him their ideas about casting and producing the movie. The picture was to be "great" in every way. Super-colossal, super, super-colossal, it had to be Miss Everything. There had to be one house as elegant and fine and rich and huge and magnolia-shaded as ninety percent of future audiences expected.

I wrote memos and more memos; I read inter-office communications; I argued, attended conferences, pointed out paragraphs from the book. Both Selznick and Menzies agreed that I was probably right and undoubtedly sincere but certain concessions must be made to the ideas of the public, and Twelve Oaks must be a mansion.

In vain I pleaded that if the locale were Charleston or Mobile more elegance and refinement might be permitted; I quoted from the book: "On the coast life had mellowed; here it was young and lusty and new."

Mr. Selznick settled the matter with a remark:

"Oh, stop worrying! Your Georgia friends will look at Twelve Oaks and sigh and say, 'Look, isn't it lovely? It's just like the one my grandfather had that Sherman burned.'"

And Twelve Oaks was constructed to follow the original plan. But the argument about cotton chopping was to go on and on. A third and fourth inter-office communication invited me to look over the location for cotton chopping. My third and fourth memos reiterated my original reply on the subject: "You can't chop cotton on the fifteenth of April."

In May I went to Chico for some incidental shots. Chico was in the northwestern part of California and the exteriors would be filmed without showing pepper trees or eucalyptus trees. The area had a topography much like that of North Georgia with fine oak trees, rolling hills, and rocky streams. By scattering red brick dust over the ground we could produce the proper resemblance to the landscape of Clayton County.

The location was some six or eight miles from the town of Chico and we rode to work in buses, leaving the hotel at seven each morning and returning at seven that evening, eating lunch on location and having a fine lazy time in the bright sunshine. Our script called for cloud effects in the backgrounds of the shots and by the time May comes in the northern section of California, there is scarcely a cloud as big as a raindrop to be seen. So we read books, played games, slept, rode horseback, wandered about the area, killed time as effectively as possible during the days, packed up and went home at night, to await a repeat on the whole thing the next day. No telephones, no interoffice communications; it was delightful. That is, it was fine until the day a messenger came from out of town to tell me an important call waited for me at the hotel. I was to call the operator at Los Angeles as soon as possible.

I called. Mr. Selznick wanted to know if I had ever approved the ground for the cotton chopping scene:

Once more I said: "You can't chop cotton in mid-April."

Then I went back to the location to do a little work; for the dogwood blossoms had arrived. Thousands of them had been made in the studio workshop and shipped up to Chico; the "green man" wanted me to tell him whether they would be effective if tied to peach trees.

For that matter, thousands and thousands of apple blossoms had been made in the studio workshop; for the shooting at Chico had been postponed so long that the dry season had set in; the apple trees, like the dogwoods, had long since finished their blossoming; the grass had turned brown with the drought. (It never rains in California!)

But don't think the art director was bothered by brown grass. The special effects man sprayed the grass with green paint and he produced cowslips and other meadow flowers by spraying with yellow and blue paint. (We called the man Maxfield Parrish.)

After some three weeks, a few clouds blew up and we made the shots and I returned to my desk in Culver City. My first inter-office memo asked me to go look at a cotton chopping location. The memo said someone had suggested that newly sprouted green peas looked like cotton newly sprouted and would I give my opinion.

I dictated the usual reply, telephoned Transportation, and drove to the area designated. I came back to the office, wrote another memo: Yes, young peas were dicotyledonous and did look much like young, tender cotton plants. But the peas had been broadcast, while cotton is planted in rows. The field would have to be plowed, rows run on a curve; it would have to be dusted with red earth. I suggested that the art director should read once more Miss Mitchell's description of plowed fields, indicated pages and paragraphs. I added a final paragraph. "You don't chop cotton in mid-April."

Then I hurried out to Forty Acres, where Director Victor Fleming was tearing his hair because the front porch of the Butler house in Atlanta had a rose vine climbing upon it and the roses were in bloom. What time of year was this scene supposed to be, he demanded of me. Wasn't that date set as of late September? What the hell business did I have letting the green man have blossoms on the rose bushes in autumn? He wanted an autumn atmosphere.

I explained that fall roses in Georgia are as prolific as spring roses and that the only thing wrong with the scene was the size of the blossoms; Californian roses are the size of cabbages and the Georgia roses in GWTW days were much smaller.

But he did not mind the rise of the roses; the effect was good. He did want the scene to be autumnal, however, and roses were spoiling the whole thing. He was cross with the green man and demanded brown leaves to float over the porch in the autumn breeze. We had a recess of several hours while the green man got oak leaves ready. I played sinking battleships with Vivien Leigh while we waited. The telephone called me. Mr. Selznick wanted to know if I could tell the field man just how the ground should be plowed for the cotton chopping scene. I said I could but would he please remember that you don't chop cotton in mid-April.

The green man handed the brown leaves to the grip or gaffer or whoever it is the union lets handle brown leaves, and, as the camera ground away, Vivien sat on the porch and watched Bonnie riding her pony, and an occasional brown leaf drifted across the pink roses. The drift had to be corrected several times because the electric fan which made the breeze to drift the leaves blew too hard or floated the leaves in the wrong direction. Finally, the fan was turned off and the leaves drifted in the right fashion, borne by the light California breeze.

The same breeze lulled me. I forgot about cotton chopping. In fact, I didn't think of it again until three weeks later when the ubiquitous inter-office communication asked me to go look at the cotton chopping site once more, this time to see if the peas had outgrown the chopping stage. They had. The tendrils were 18 inches long. I so reported in an inter-office communication.

There was another interim with no reference to the cotton situation. I devoted my attention to the technicalities of a scene on a river boat that was taking Rhett and Scarlett on their honeymoon trip down the Mississippi to New Orleans. Knowing less than nothing about a river boat I was hard put to find anything to criticize and I fretted about possible mistakes which I would not discover until too late.

In fact, I almost made one error. The director had opened his mouth to yell "Quiet," when I realized that a heavy blanket was pulled up over the lovely Scarlett as she lay in her bunk—and the time was July and the locale, the lower Mississippi.

I got the blanket off.

The sun, powerful electric lights, shone down on the river, a huge shallow tub of water, just outside camera range. An electric fan stirred the waters; reflections danced upon the walls of Scarlett's cabin.

The light bulb over the telephone turned red, a fifth assistant director answered the phone and motioned to me; Selznick wanted to see me.

I walked the four or five blocks to his office, wondering what now.

"Would it be possible to trim the tendrils off those peas and prepare that field so it might still be used for the cotton chopping scene?" he asked.

"This is where I came in, six months ago," I thought, wearily. But aloud I said:

"You can't chop cotton in the middle of April."

I left Hollywood in July, traveled up the coast and spent six weeks on the return to Georgia, devoting my time to forgetting the trials of the past six months. But I never freed myself from the shadow of cotton chopping until I saw the premiere of *Gone With the Wind* in Atlanta in December, 1939.

When the picture was over I knew it was so exciting that nobody would have cared if we had chopped cotton in mid-April.

GONE WITH THE WIND

The Motion Picture

In spite of much coaxing from David O. Selznick, producer of *Gone With the Wind*, Margaret Mitchell steadfastly refused to go to Hollywood to supervise the making of the movie from her famous book. She would have nothing to do with it, she told Hollywood. Hence, Mr. Selznick selected three Southerners to aid him in making the production faithful to Southern tradition; Wilbur Kurtz of Atlanta, to advise on scenes and historical material; Will Price of Magnolia, Mississippi, to aid in coaching Vivien Leigh in Southern speech; and Susan Myrick of Macon to advise on Southern manners, customs and accent.

The millions of people in the United States and in many other nations, who had read and loved the story of Scarlett and Rhett, and the tale of the South's courage in the face of defeat in war and the trials of the Reconstruction Era, had been asking for three years: "When will the movie be made? What will it be like?" And those concerned with the cinema production faced a grave responsibility, when, on January 26, 1939, the first day's shooting began—a schedule which was to go on for 140 days.

Among the many taboos, fears and hopes expressed by a concerned public, the one which raised the loudest voice was concerned with the problem of "The Southern Accent." Mr. Selznick agreed with his advisors that there is no such thing as "The Southern Accent," that the accent of the Southerner has many varieties; that your Tidewater-Virginia speech is little akin to that of say, mid-Alabama, and the accent of your Charlestonian is more like that of a native of Brunswick, Maine, than like the dialect of a North Mississippian or a man from New Orleans. So, happily the matter of accent was a compromise; the actors would use good diction such as one is accustomed to hear from stage and screen, and the feel of the South would be given by the use of Southern idiom and the pronunciation of certain words in the fashion of your middle Georgian, who says "cawfee" for "coffee" and "mawning" for "morning." The book is filled with Southern idiom and Sidney

Howard, in his script writing, was careful to use the conversation as Margaret Mitchell had put it down.

If there is one thing common to Southern accents it is the lack of a rolling "r" (though in some mountain sections of the South a definite "r" is apparent in the speech). Southern children learn the alphabet, "l, m, n, o, p, q, ah" (not r-r), as, of course, do many youngsters of New England areas. Since Vivien Leigh and Leslie Howard were Britishers, they said "ah" for "r" in the Southern fashion. Olivia de Havilland's speech was also minus an "r," which left Clark Gable the only leading player whose speech retained a vestige of the mid-Western "r." It took only a brief few days for the "sound of the South" to permeate the speech of everybody on the GWTW set, from extras, lighting experts, camera men and hairdressers, to the stars of the show.

The staccato of the British speech of Vivien Leigh and Leslie Howard soon changed to the more leisurely tenor of the speech of the people of the Southern United States; the British "bean" turned quickly to the American "been" and the British "t" became a "d." "Theah hasn't been any fun at any pahdy..." said Scarlett O'Hara on the momentous first day of the shooting, as she sat on the steps at Tara, flirting with the Tarleton twins.

The speech of the Negroes of the play was modeled on that of the Uncle Remus book, and Hattie McDaniel, as Mammy, and Butterfly McQueen, as Prissy, soon became adept at the Middle Georgia plantation Negro dialect.

The first script for GWTW was completed February 20, 1937, but the final shooting script was not finished until February 27, 1939, a script which contained 20,017 words of dialogue and 685 script scenes. But preliminary shooting began before Miss Leigh had been chosen for the role of Scarlett. The burning of their military stores and supplies by the Confederate troops, prior to their evacuation of Atlanta, was filmed December 10, 1938, almost one year before the premiere in Atlanta. A total of 4,400 people were employed in the making of the movie which cost nearly 4 million dollars, grossed 37 million, won 10 academy awards and had the largest aggregate audience of any movie ever made, 100 million in the United States alone.

There were hundreds of small problems of Southern manners and customs of the Sixties and Seventies to be solved each day as the shooting went on: What did a match look like in 1864? What sort of wedding ring would Scarlett wear? Did nurses use thermometers when they took care of wounded Confederate soldiers in Atlanta? What does a scuppernong arbor look like? Could the Negroes chop cotton on the afternoon before the barbecue at Twelve Oaks, the day when it was announced that Mr. Lincoln had declared war? Would Spanish moss hang on the cedar trees at Tara? These and scores of other questions were studied with consummate patience always with the careful attention to detail which was the mark of David O. Selznick's genius.

So, it came about that after four years of breathless waiting a few hundred lucky people saw the premiere of *Gone With the Wind* at Loew's Grand Theater in Atlanta December 15, 1939, and the acclaim was tremendous. It was a premiere "heard round the world" as Atlanta put on its best show of Southern hospitality, as a million people jammed the sidewalks of the city to see the stars of the movie, in person, as a brilliant ball for the celebrities ranked with the finest of all social events, and Atlanta and the nation paid homage to Margaret Mitchell who had written a great book, now come alive again in a great movie.

The success of the movie is due to a good story, good direction and infinite attention to detail. The combination of these three resulted in *Gone With the Wind*'s being the greatest movie of all time. After 15 years, the movie is almost as popular as when it was issued in 1939. As of now, it has been seen by more than a hundred million Americans and by an equal number abroad, having been shown in every country of the world with the exception of Russia and her satellites. There is every reason to believe *Gone With the Wind* will continue its extraordinary career as long as motion pictures exist.

Margaret Mitchell, **The Atlanta Public Library, 1954, pp. 27-30.**

WHAT A BOOK!

Saturday marked the 20th anniversary of the publication of the remarkable novel *Gone With the Wind*, which has outsold any novel of this century.

Released June 30, 1936, the book sold out its initial 10,000 copies to the Book of the Month Club, and subsequent printings sold so fast the millionth copy was presented to Margaret Mitchell at Christmas of that year.

I remember seeing the millionth copy at the home of Peggy Mitchell and her husband John Marsh. The book was bound in red leather with gold lettering on the cover, and a special flyleaf which said the Macmillan Company presented the millionth copy to the author with gratitude and appreciation.

The spring previous to the publication of GWTW, Peggy came to Macon to talk at the Macon Writers' Club breakfast, one of the few public appearances she ever made, for Peggy was a shy person and did not like to be lionized. (See Appendix III .) Those who had the good fortune to hear her speech in the spring of 1936 remember it as the most entertaining and delightful thing they ever encountered, and they remember her as a retiring and modest person who thought the publisher should print only 5,000 copies for the initial printing. She knew a few hundred people would buy the book out of friendship, she said, but she shuddered to think of how many books would be left on the publishers' hands if they dared print 10,000 copies.

I remember writing to my sister (Allie M. Bowden) who was living then in Oregon, telling her of the book and suggesting she should read it when it came out, since I had known Peggy long enough to know whatever she wrote was bound to be fascinating. It was laughable in the light of the eight million copies of the book sold since that time, to remember my sister's request to the librarian in the city where she was living. She asked that the library buy a copy of the book, explaining that it would probably be somewhat popular and requesting that it be reserved for her when it should arrive at the library.

Another of my sisters (Katie M. Lowerre), living in (Rome) New York, asked her book store to get her a copy, and explained her extravagance to her husband by saying she "wanted to help out Sue's friend, Margaret Mitchell."

During the past 20 years, *Gone With the Wind* has been printed in 30 languages and 40 countries. More than four million copies have been sold in the United States.

The movie version of the story has enjoyed, also, a fabulous popularity in many countries; in London, it ran for four and a half years. The picture cost around five million dollars to produce, and has grossed more than $40 million.

Macon Telegraph, July 2, 1956

MY FRIENDS HAVE GONE WITH THE WIND

"Fiddle-dee-dee! War, war, war! This war talk's spoiling all the fun—"

Scarlett O'Hara was talking to the Tarleton twins on the front porch at Tara, her dark curling hair, fair skin, and blue-green eyes lovely above her hoopskirted dress of fine white lawn, trimmed with lace insertion and fine tucks. The handsome twins, long-legged, high-booted, each holding a mint julep, lounged near.

It was January 1939, and Selznick International Pictures was shooting the first scene in *Gone With the Wind*, a movie destined to become the favorite of millions and win innumerable "firsts." It was an exciting day for everybody, especially for me. I had gone to Culver City, California, from Macon, Georgia, to serve as technical adviser on accents, manners, and customs of the Old South; and I was scared stiff.

The job had come to me largely through my friendship with Margaret Mitchell, whom I had known for many years, and she had talked much to me about keeping the movie "true to the South." I wanted to do the best possible job as an advisor, not only through pride in my work but because of my affection and admiration for Margaret Mitchell.

I was particularly concerned with accent. My contract said I was to "teach the Southern accent," and I knew there was no such thing as *the* Southern accent. There are many Southern accents. The Charlestonian (Rhett Butler was one) does not speak with the same accent as does the Atlantan (Scarlett O'Hara lived in Atlanta). And though the Charleston accent is closely related to that of the Savannah native, the speech of the Tidewater Virginian (Ashley Wilkes) is different from either, in spite of similarities. A girl from Montgomery, Alabama, has a different accent from the girl who was born and reared in Birmingham, and a mountain woman from Tennessee speaks in a very different way from the native of the Mississippi Delta country.

Most of all, I was scared Producer David O. Selznick would insist upon an accent such as I had heard on various screen recordings and radio programs—a phony, exaggerated speech assumed by a "Yankee" who endeavored to speak in what he considered a "Southern drawl." I knew the South was likely to fire on Fort Sumter again if Rhett said to Scarlett, "Honey child, Ah'm go' thro mah ahms rat aroun' yo' neck."

But I need not have been afraid. Mr. Selznick was a great man, with a keen understanding, a bright mind, a magnificent sense of pageantry, and a passion for perfection. He knew millions of people had read *Gone With the Wind* and loved it and that his movie must be true in every way to the book. I think no other producer could have made so faithful a presentation of Margaret Mitchell's magnificent story of the South, the War Between the States, and the "Tragic Era" of Reconstruction. Mr. Selznick readily agreed with me on accents. We decided to have the performers use the good stage English that people have grown to expect on screen and on stage.

We would get the effect of Southern accent by the use of Southern idiom (in which Miss Mitchell's book abounds) and the pronunciation of certain words in the manner of the average Mid-Georgian: "Cawfee," for example, and "lawg" and "own." Your average Mid-Georgian is likely to say he sat "own a lawg and drank his cawfee."

Of course, we'd have no "R" in the speech. If there is one thing common to the varieties of Southern accent it is the absence of an "R." Your southern child learns his alphabet, "L, M, N, O, P, Q, ah"—not "P, Q, R." Both Leslie Howard and Vivien Leigh, being British, said "ah" for "R" as did Olivia de Havilland, who had long since acquired the good diction required for a top-bracket stage performance. But Clark Gable still had a hint of the Midwest in his speech, and I delighted in coaching him to say:

"I can't afford a four-door Ford."

Not "four-r door-r For-rd," I insisted. "And if you say, 'I kaint affode a fo-do Fode,' I'll fetch out my grandpa's Confederate rifle."

My contract called for me to teach "the Southern accent" to both white and colored performers and there was no question about the accent of the Negro performers; they would speak in the accents of Uncle Remus, the speech of the Middle Georgia plantation Negro of 1860. Hattie McDaniel, a native of Tennessee, already knew just how Mammy would talk, and Miss McDaniel was largely responsible for the fine accent of Butterfly McQueen, who made such a hit in her role of Prissy. Miss McQueen had never been south of the Potomac and knew nothing of the Uncle Remus accent. Without Mammy's aid, I doubt I should ever have been able to get Prissy's speech right. Not that I could blame Miss McQueen; it is difficult to read dialect, and Sidney Howard's script had taken the speech of the Negroes from Miss Mitchell's book verbatim.

"Miss Scar-rlett, I is skair-rt ter-r go ter-r der-r deepo," Prissy would read, and it took patient effort to get from her: "Miss Scahlett, Ah is skeered tuh go tuh de deepo. Dey's daid fokes down deah."

But Prissy achieved a good accent and few persons who have seen *Gone With the Wind* will ever forget the little Negro girl who "didn't know nuthin' bout birthin' babies," but told Miss Scarlett when Miss Mellie's baby was coming:

"Ma say if you put a knife under de bed hit'll cut de pain."

Shortly after my arrival in Hollywood I was scheduled to go to the home of Leslie Howard for an accent lesson, an appointment which resulted later on in a vast amount of kidding for me. I arrived at Mr. Howard's house at noon; a maid answered the doorbell, invited me in, said Mr. 'Oward was "on the trunk" and would be available in a little while. She was veddy British and veddy Cockney in her speech, and she chatted as she brought me the morning "pyper" and offered me a cup of tea. I waited some 45 minutes for Mr. Howard, wondering the while about the strange British custom of sitting on a trunk. Presently he came tripping down the stairs, very handsome in light-blue slacks and matching shirt open at the neck, his reddish-gold hair shining in the light. He apologized for keeping me waiting, explaining he'd "bean" talking on the trunk to London," so that I realized "on the trunk" meant on the long distance telephone. He said since it was quite late perhaps I would stay for lunch with him, and naturally I accepted his kind invitation.

I discovered that there were to be other guests—all of them important and all of them British: John Balderston and John Van Druten and Vivien Leigh and Laurence Olivier. I was overwhelmed at the presence of so many celebrities and kept my feeble Southern mouth closed all through lunch, while I listened to British accent and talk of Shakespeare folios and such.

When I got back to the main office, the director wanted to know how my accent lesson went. I told him with a strong British accent that I had had a wonderful time, really; for I have an unfortunate way of imitating the speech of anybody I chance to be with. You'd almost have believed I'd "bean" a student at Oxford or Cambridge. The director and all his aides howled and offered to pay for a "trunk call" to Georgia for me, so I could get back my Southern accent. I resolved the matter by reading a half dozen Uncle Remus tales aloud.

Manners and customs of the Old South gave me little bother as the movie progressed. It was not difficult to answer most of the questions. What sort of wedding ring would Scarlett have? How would Scarlett sign a check? How was Mammy's head rag tied? Would the house servants at Tara be present for family prayers? What did a scuppernong vine look like? How would the girls carry with them to the barbecue the dresses they'd don for the dancing? If somebody asked me a question I couldn't answer, I could always get help from Wilbur Kurtz, an Atlanta man who served as historian for the movie. Occasionally, Will Price of Magnolia, Mississippi, one of the advisors on speech, would ask me if I would permit something or other, saying he was doubtful about it. I loved telling him in the words of Scarlett O'Hara that he was just a "coarse Westerner from Mississippi" and he wouldn't know.

There was much kidding on the sets from day to day; there had to be, for the day began at 7 a.m. and often was not over until 11 p.m., and some laughter was necessary to keep us from going nuts. Everybody had a fine laugh when Ed Boyle, who was in charge of sets, asked me with a serious face to please come have a look at Belle Watling's place to see if I thought it a faithful representation of such an establishment as Belle's. I told him to be sure to have a parrot on the set.

When I had a note from the head office asking that I go to the hospital and select a baby to be photographed for the newborn Bonnie, daughter of Scarlett and Rhett, the crew demanded that I be certain the baby cried with a Southern accent. Everybody relaxed and had a good laugh when Director Victor Fleming, between takes, got one of the prop men to slip a large stone in the bed with Melanie, so that when Clark Gable lifted her, blanket-wrapped, to carry her to the wagon for the trip back to Tara, he found her weighing about 140 pounds instead of her normal 98 or so.

Though we clowned often and had a measure of fun during the seven months I worked as advisor on the movie, all of us, cast and crew, felt somehow that here was something extraordinary, a great movie, faithful to a great book. A record for that date, the movie cost $4 million, a sum which has been returned many fold. Last counts placed returns at more than $60 million (in early 1967), and when *Gone With the Wind* shows again in October 1967, there'll undoubtedly be a sizeable increase.

The premiere of the picture was in Atlanta, December 15, 1939, and Lawdy, Miss Scarlett, what a whoop-de-do! If the Confederate Army had had as many soldiers as there were people on the streets of Atlanta to see the *Gone With the Wind* celebrities, the South would have won the war. Vivien Leigh and her intended, Laurence Olivier; Clark Gable and his wife of that date, Carol Lombard; Olivia de Havilland, Leslie Howard, Laura Hope Crews, and a glamorous assortment of other stars were on hand for the ball which the Atlanta Junior League sponsored the evening before the premier, and people who had invitations were the most envied persons in the world. Margaret Mitchell captivated the stars when she entertained them simply in her apartment. And when the premier showing of the picture was over, she spoke briefly to the enchanted audience in the theater, saying she considered it a great movie and offered congratulations to cast and producer and director, alike.

A new generation will see *Gone With the Wind* in October 1967, for the picture was last shown in 1961 to celebrate the hundredth anniversary of the start of the War Between the States. Much drama and tragedy has passed by since Miss Mitchell's great book was made into a movie. The tiny author, herself, is dead, killed by a taxi driver on the streets of Atlanta; her husband, John Marsh, is dead also. Dead are Leslie Howard, Vivien Leigh, Clark Gable, Laura Hope Crews, David O. Selznick, Director Victor Fleming, Hattie McDaniel—sometimes I think everybody's dead except me and Prissy.

But the movie will live forever. I am proud to have had a part in the production. In fact, I am like Prissy when she went to find Cap'n Butler to ask him to get a horse and wagon to take Miss Scarlett and Miss Mellie back to Tara. "Cap'n Butler," she said, "Miss Mellie done had her baby." And when he asked if she and Miss Scarlett brought that baby without any help from a doctor, Prissy said,

"Well, Miss Scarlett, she holp me some, but hit was mostly me."

I feel that in making the marvelous movie *Gone With the Wind*, Miss Leigh and Miss Mitchell and Mr. Selznick and others "holp me some, but hit was mostly me."

Southern Living, Vol. 2, No. 9, October 1962, pp. 30-33, 46

JAPANESE GWTW

Fleeing Atlanta as it burned

Peggy Mitchell had a vivid imagination, as the Maconites who were lucky enough to know her well can all testify. But I venture a guess that Peggy, in her wildest flights of imagination, never thought of a Japanese Rhett Butler. Nor, for that matter, a Japanese Prissy.

But, as many of you know, it has happened; the Japanese have produced a GWTW with Japanese Southern Gentlemen, complete with red-haired Tarleton twins, all turned out in wing collars and Confederate uniforms. A friend gave me a photograph that showed Mammy and Prissy, with Oriental eyes and black face, and a Clark Gable who seemed to be about five feet, four.

Gable, who in the minds of all Americans is Rhett Butler, the dashing Charlestonian who smuggled things through in times of "de Wah" and had lovely green bonnets and bottles of Florida Water for Miss Scarlett, is a favorite in Japan as well as in the Western World. He wears black riding boots—in the Japanese version of GWTW—and takes long strides to create the illusion of height—or so it is reported.

Al Ricketts, who writes a column for *Stars and Strips*, reports that the Southern soldiers ham it up in the best Japanese tradition, staggering, reeling, screaming and "disintegrating right before your very eyes."

The show lasts four and a half hours, with a 40-minute intermission. If it's that long, the show might even include some of the scenes we shot in Hollywood and then edited out. I wonder if the Japanese version shows the arrival of Prissy at Tara with Dilcey thanking Miss Scarlett for asking Mr. O'Hara to purchase the wife and daughter of Pork.

The Japanese version might even include some background on Rhett and show what it was he did that caused him to be expelled from West Point. I have wondered about that since I first read GWTW in 1936.

One of the most marvelous pictures in the book is that which Peggy Mitchell painted as she wrote of the funeral of Gerald O'Hara. I always wished the movie Mr. Selznick made might have included that scene. But even in a Hollywood movie, you can't have everything, I guess.

I understand the customers at the Japanese production can rent transistorized gadgets which will provide a running English translation. Lawdy, I wonder what the Japanese actor says when he is speaking Scarlett's favorite expletive, "God's nightgown." And what sort of Southern speech comes out on the translation? I wish I could hear it.

Macon Telegraph, February 20, 1967

PRIVATE LIFE (OF MARGARET MITCHELL)

Stories about famous persons tend to grow to such size as to be almost unrecognizable, and I begin to realize, now, what Margaret Mitchell meant when she asked me, back in 1939, to please burn all the letters she had ever written me and all she might write later. She hated to think, she said, that when she was long dead some callow sophomore on an English assignment would read in a library some letters she had written, letters never meant for eyes other than those of the close friend to whom she had written.

As the world heaped honors upon her after a million copies of her GWTW had been sold within six months of its publication, the people were filled with curiosity about the author of the book that everybody "sat up all night to finish." And Peggy had some wry laughs over stories, born out of thin air, which circulated about her: "I could stand it when people said my husband or my father really wrote the book," she said. "I didn't mind much when I heard I had gone blind—I almost did from reading proof—but I was slightly upset when I heard I had a peg leg."

In a recent issue of the *Saturday Review*, Cleveland Amory devotes several columns to Margaret Mitchell, most of his material taken from the book written by Finis Farr, whom Mr. Amory call a "friend" of Peggy's. That ought to amuse her if she chances to hear of it through the news channels of some cherubims. Mr. Farr told many stories of Peggy's private life which I believe would have made her cringe. She thought her private life ought to be private and she would not like to have intimate details of her life spread on a printed page.

According to Mr. Amory, Margaret kept a loaded pistol beside her bed every night of her life "until the news of her first husband's death" came to her.

Well, I spent a good many weekends as a guest at the Mitchell-Marsh apartment in Atlanta, and since there was only one bedroom,

John Marsh slept in the day bed in the living room while Peggy and I had the bed in the bedroom. If she had a pistol anywhere near that bed I never saw it. And my eye sight was pretty good, back then.

One thing Mr. Amory said I agree with: "You have to look hard in Atlanta or elsewhere to find the real story of this remarkable woman."

Perhaps the best story about her that has been printed is that in Mr. Farr's book, but I regret the publication of letters and stories about Miss Mitchell which she regarded as strictly personal.

———————————

Macon Telegraph, August 10, 1967

ALICIA RHETT

When Selznick International Pictures was making *Gone With the Wind*, in 1939, a lovely young woman from Charleston, South Carolina, arrived to play the role of India Wilkes. The Charleston girl's name was Alicia Rhett and of course that name didn't detract from her glamour.

When Alicia arrived with that most delightful accent of the Coastal areas, which seems particularly strong in your native Charlestonian, everybody on the set, except me, almost went overboard.

Did Mr. Selznick wish me to work with Miss Rhett on accent? No, indeed. He thought I was a little presumptuous to want to do anything about an accent from the Deep South. But once he heard her talk, he changed his tune. He scarcely understood what she said. Mr. Menzies, an Englishman who was art director for the movie, said Miss Rhett's speech was so much like that of his Scotch-Irish grandmother that it fairly made him homesick to hear her.

A rather quiet young woman, apparently a little shy, Alicia spent much time with her sketch pad. She sketched cast and crew and never made a production of it—just sketched for her own amusement and not to attract attention to herself or her drawings.

For many a long year I've wondered what has become of that lovely girl from Charleston. I've just found out. A friend sent me a tear sheet from the *Charleston Evening Post* which told of Alicia, today. She is a "rather shy, friendly gentlewoman about Charleston, now" the reporter (Warren Koon) wrote. She is "painting remarkable portraits and living graciously in her warm, comfortable home downtown."

There was "almost dancing in the streets in Charleston when Selznick announced that three neophytic Southern Belles would be given parts in the movie. One was a college beauty queen from Alabama (Maybelle Merriwether), one was a Sears Roebuck sales girl from New Orleans (friend of Scarlett's) and the other was shy, petite Alicia Rhett of Charleston," the reporter said.

Obviously an admirer of the ways of Miss Rhett, Mr. Koon continued: "Alicia Rhett is a genteel Southern lady who did not then, nor does she now, like notoriety. Quietly ensconced in her house, Alicia Rhett is a successful portrait painter, working in a second floor studio which captures the northern light, a constant which is best from an artistic viewpoint.

"She is a petite, gracious woman with brown hair cut shorter than the style of 1940 when she was India Wilkes, and she smiles a great deal, an honest, wide smile showing perfect, white teeth and a genuine happiness with humanity."

Alicia dismisses any talk of GWTW with a wave of her hand, and a "non committal 'All that is gone'," the reporter concludes. "She is 29 years away from the sullen, embittered India Wilkes portrayed in GWTW."

———————————

Macon Telegraph, February 1968

PRISSY

It is sometimes difficult to distinguish between fact and fancy, and right now is one of the times I'm trying to make the distinction—with small success I might say.

In the *New York Times* section on the drama and art and the cinema and such, there appeared an article recently about Butterfly McQueen, the woman who played the role of Prissy in GWTW, and now playing on the stage at the Bert Wheeler Theater in New York. A man who signed himself Guy Flatley wrote the piece about Butterfly and right from the first paragraph he had me wondering. Said he:

"Who could ever forget Prissy, that sweet simpering servant girl who caused Miss Scarlett O'Hara to lose her cool and Melanie to almost lose her baby?"

For that matter, who said Mellie almost lost the baby?

Well, Mr. Guy goes on to say that "Miss McQueen was born poor 57 years ago in the Deep South." The way I heard it—and who is to say which publicity man is right?—the way I heard it in Hollywood, Miss McQueen was a Harlem product; she had never been South of the Potomac nor west of the Mississippi until she went to California to play the role in GWTW. She told me that, herself. And the way she pronounced the dialect words that Margaret Mitchell had put into the mouth of Prissy, you'd never have believed she had been born in the Deep South.

Nevertheless, Mr. Guy quotes her as saying, "There are plenty of Prissys in the world today. You can see them standing in the doorways down South. They don't even want to be educated. In the South the Negroes have been beasts of burden. Our heads are made of cotton in the South. We work all week and get dressed up on Sundays in pretty dresses to go to church."

Well, in case Prissy DID get born in the Deep South and observe the ways of black and whites down here, she must not have observed very closely, or she'd know white people work all week, too, and dressed up on Sundays to go to church.

About her time in Hollywood, she said, according to Mr. Guy: "I found it disappointing when I began working with white people. There was no hunger for elegance that you find in so many Negroes." She added—"And you can sum up the war in Vietnam in two words: white supremacy."

Miss McQueen revealed her new romance to Mr. Guy. She told him: "I will probably marry in Africa. I like my OWN men." (The emphasis is hers.)

Macon Telegraph, Aug 22, 1968

AUGUSTA'S PRISSY

I am all mixed up—or Hollywood is, or somebody. When I spent some seven months as a technical adviser on the making of the movie *Gone With the Wind*, I was told that Butterfly McQueen, the high-voiced Negro girl who played Prissy, was a native of New York and had never been south of the Potomac River.

Now comes one Chris Brady, who writes a column for the *Augusta Chronicle-Herald*, who declares Butterfly McQueen has "come home to her native Augusta for a three-month vacation."

All this time I thought Butterfly was a Yankee.

Prissy, writes Brady, "you may remember as being slightly hare-brained and afraid of almost everything, including in order of importance, Scarlett, child-birth, gunfire and Yankees."

Now, I shall not argue with Mr. Brady, nor with Butterfly McQueen, if they insist that she is a native of Augusta, but I have a sneaking notion that a smart agent or publicity man dreamed up the idea of Prissy as a native of Augusta, thinking it would make good copy for Augusta papers when Butterfly McQueen went there to visit and to sing nightly at a restaurant.

Mr. Brady says Butterfly attended the Walker Baptist School and St. Benedict's in Augusta, and quotes her as giving credit to two of her former teachers for giving her helping hands toward her career as an actress.

Well, howcome the smart publicity men at Culver City, where GWTW was filmed, failed to discover that Prissy was a Southerner! I remember they tried to put it over that the little girl who played Bonnie, daughter of Rhett and Scarlett, was from the South. It turned out she was from southern California.

So, it seems to me they missed a good bet when they did not play up Prissy as a native of Augusta.

If Prissy was born in Augusta, she certainly outgrew her native accent speedily. Far as I could tell, when I was endeavoring to help her speak with a Southern accent in GWTW, she had never been anywhere in the Deep South. Matter of fact, if it had not been for the help I got from Mammy (Hattie McDaniel, who was a native of Tennessee) I think I should never have been able to get Prissy to sound right.

Her voice was as full or R-R-R's as if she came from upper New York State and had associated mostly with those whose accents were derived from German ancestors.

"Miss Scar-r-rlett," she'd say, "I don't know nothing about bir-r-r-rthing babies."

It took a heap of doing for Mammy and me to persuade her to sound like Prissy would have sounded if she had been Aunt Pittypat's maid in real life.

Macon Telegraph, **date unknown**

Editor's note: In a 1989 interview with Gary Swint then director of the Augusta-Richmond County Public Library, and reported in *The Augusta Chronicle* on April 10, 2011, McQueen stated that she was born in Tampa, Florida on January 8, 1911. She said she moved to Augusta, but did not know how old she was at the time of the move.

MOVIE ITEMS GO ON BLOCK

With thousands of catalogues sold at $10.00 each, the auction of Metro-Goldwyn-Mayer's objects, accumulated over the past 56 years for use in the movies they made (about 2,000 pictures) should bring in a considerable sum of money.

The announcement of the auction brought some memories for me, memories of working on technical matters at the making of *Gone With the Wind*, more than 30 years ago. GWTW was made by Selznick Studios, located not far from the MGM studios at Culver City, but one or two scenes of the movie of the Sixties were shot at MGM. I can't tell you why. We, the hired help at Selznick's, figured maybe it was because Mrs. Selznick was a daughter of a member of the MGM firm.

Anyway, it was at the MGM studio that we shot the scene where Bonnie, the idol of her father, Rhett Butler, was killed riding her pony in a jump.

Wearing her blue riding outfit, the blue because her name was Bonnie Blue and because the suit made her eyes look a little blue (they were really brown) Bonnie posed innumerable times on the pony, with Clark Gable proudly looking on. The jump was shot with a "stunt man" taking the fall. He was a midget, wearing a wig and a replica of Bonnie's blue riding habit.

I've never found out why I was expected to be on hand for that particular scene. Nobody said a word, and my job was that of adviser on Southern accent. But I was delighted to be in on a scene shot at MGM and greatly pleased to have a chance to go through some of the thousands of feet of warehouse space at the studio.

The set designed for GWTW had borrowed some furniture from the MGM lot; "borrowing" was the term he used. I imagine Mr. Selznick paid a pretty penny for the "borrowing." I remember an English desk that was "borrowed" for a scene with Bonnie as a young child, enjoying a tea set her father had brought her when he retuned from one of his trips, selling contraband goods. The scene, you may be interested to know, was cut; it was one of the many scenes cut from the final picture in order to shorten the time for the showing.

The objects for sale in the MGM auction included such fabulous things as Judy Garland's slippers, worn into the Land of Oz; Norma Shearer's costumes worn in *Marie Antoinette*; a 1931 Ford roadster with a rumble seat, that was driven by Mickey Rooney in 15 Andy Hardy movies; the panties worn by Greta Garbo in *Mata Hari*; Elizabeth Taylor's rich brocades and Jean Harlow's costumes glittering with sequins.

MGM had stored away objects as faithfully as any grandmother, only MGM had a lot more space that Grandma's attic afforded.

_____

Macon Telegraph, May 7, 1970

TARA FILMED IN CALIFORNIA

Thirty-one years have gone by since *Gone With the Wind* was first shown on the screen in Atlanta, and it is just about 35 years ago that Margaret Mitchell's Pulitzer prize novel made its appearance, but arguments and discussion about the book and the movie go on with almost as much fervor as those of 30 years ago.

Everybody over 45 remembers how Miss Mitchell was harassed by telephone, telegram, and letters from people who primarily wanted to know if Scarlett and Rhett were ever reunited. The petite author declared she had to stay at home, she dared not go downtown lest some character leap at her from behind a telephone post to tell her about the sequel she ought to write to the story of the beautiful and proud Scarlett and her husband, the proud and obstinate Rhett Butler.

It was only last week that a young high school student wrote to ask if I would favor her by reading the sequel she has written. And, a short time ago, I had the 20th letter about whether any part of GWTW was filmed in Charleston, SC. The letters have all been written this past year and all written by tourists complaining that they had been told at Boone Hall that much of the picture GWTW was filmed at that home, located near US Highway 17 in Mount Pleasant.

The other day, I had a letter from a Dublin woman who enclosed a clipping from the Charleston *Courier-Journal* about Boone Hall; the two reporters who had toured the home had been given false information, which they cleared up by revealing a statement made by Raymond Klune, a retired motion picture executive living in Hollywood. He was production chief for the film and he declared:

"Nothing in *Gone With the Wind* was filmed outside of California with the exception of one shot of a riverboat on the Mississippi River."

My correspondent asked me to "shed some light" on the matter. All I can do is agree with Mr. Klune. I spent nearly eight months in California while the film was being made and I am dead certain that the shots were made in California, not in Charleston or in any area nearby.

The reporters for the Charleston newspaper said they were told among other things, the scene on the front porch at Tara where Scarlett and the Twins sat for the opening scene of the picture was shot at Boone Hall.

Mrs. Milton Angelakos, who wrote me about the report in the *Courier* said she is a native of South Carolina and she "dislikes the idea of a tourist being given false information."

So do I, Mrs. Angelakos, and I feel sure the report carried in the Charleston paper indicates something is going to be done about the false reports of the filming of GWTW at Boone Hall.

Macon Telegraph, **June 21, 1971**

Editor's Note: Although Margaret Mitchell never publicly answered whether or not Rhett and Scarlett re-united, Susan Myrick wrote two newspaper columns about the matter. In one, she stated that, like Mitchell, she did not know. In the other, after years of queries from GWTW fans, she gave an opinion. Both columns are given in her biography: **Susan Myrick of Gone With the Wind: An Autobiographical Biography**. See end pages for ordering information.

MEMOIR OF GWTW

Miss Sue was not only on the movie set, teaching Scarlett O'Hara how to drop her gees. She also remembers teaching David O. Selznick a thing or two.

It is January 16, 1939, nearly three years since David O. Selznick bought the movie rights to Margaret Mitchell's Pulitzer prize winning novel. In the office of George Cukor, chosen two years ago to direct GWTW, is a disconsolate group, among them, me, also chosen two years ago as technical adviser on accent, manners and customs. Mr. Selznick had just fired on Four Sumter; he had announced the shooting will begin one week from today.

Art consultants, production directors, makeup and wardrobe men, along with assistant directors, camera men, assistants to assistants, technical advisers, dialogue directors, electrician specialists, and somebody named "Mr. Ginsberg" (who is apparently vice-president in charge of holding down expenses) look as anguished as Scarlett O'Hara did when Rhett told her he "didn't give a damn." Everybody who is anybody is present except a chap named Platt who is in charge of set decorations.

Cukor opens the meeting with "Where is Platt?"

Three assistants, speaking in chorus, say Platt went back to New York three weeks ago and nobody's heard from him since. Cukor says you can't dress sets by long distance from New York to California and, by God, somebody better get Platt back in a hurry. The three men say they'll call Platt, and Mr. Ginsberg says don't five or six people call Platt, just get together and make ONE phone call.

Cukor asks Ned Lambert, head of wardrobe, if any costumes are ready and Lambert says not one, and how can he make costumes when he has no measurements for anybody and where in hell are the actors. An eager young aide says he has height-weight for Butterfly McQueen, and wardrobe says you can't make clothes by height-weight, and, besides, who knows that Butterfly will really be Prissy, and though costumes have been designed for two years he can't get started on them until he has all measurements—shoes, dresses, petticoats, and godknowswhat; and when costumes are made, they have to be okayed by Cukor and Selznick, and Miss Myrick has to say if they look "S'uthe'n," and they just can't be ready by Monday, January 23rd.

Cukor says has anybody seen Gable and there is a long silence. Mr. Ginsberg then says he's been calling Gable's agent for a week and he won't even answer the phone. Cukor says goddammit, he can't lead actors around by the hand to wardrobe and makeup and—

Assistant director Eric Stacey interrupts: Does Cukor know if all the characters for the movie have been selected yet? Cukor says he thinks so, though he knows full well the only ones who are certain are Gable and Vivien Leigh and Leslie Howard, and well maybe Mammy. (An assistant director had asked me, only this morning, what I thought about Marian Anderson for the role: "They could write in some songs for her.")

After an hour of getting no answers to anything, Cukor rises and says, anyhow, we'll start shooting Monday morning and everybody should be ready, and Ginsberg echoes "Monday morning." Stacey says, "OK, we start shooting Monday morning, but don't blame me if there is nothing to shoot Tuesday, Wednesday and Thursday."

On my way back from the meeting to my office, I meet Mr. Selznick, who asks if I think Southerners (including Margaret Mitchell) will object to his choice of Vivien Leigh, a Britisher, as Scarlett. He wonders if I have any ideas about some good publicity on the choice. I suggest that I know Mrs. Walter Douglas Lamar of Macon, who is President-General of the United Daughters of the Confederacy, and maybe I can get her to come out to Culver City and raise the Confederate flag over Selznick International Pictures with Vivien looking on.

He is ecstatic over the idea, tells me to telephone Mrs. Lamar at once, that SIP will pay all expenses and be honored by her presence.

I try for 24 hours to telephone Mrs. Lamar, finally get the information that she is out of the city and cannot be reached for three days. Before I can get this information to Mr. Selznick, I get an interoffice communication from him that says: "do nothing more about that Confederate Head's coming out here to raise the Confederate flag."

For the ten days following the meeting in Cukor's office, I listened to accents of candidates who were trying out for various roles. I heard ten Charles Hamiltons practice on "I love you, Miss Scarlett. May I—dare I, hope—" and a half dozen Belle Watlings "conversin' with Miz Wilkes"; and I worried over questions like how would Mammy's headrag be tied and how long would Prissy's skirts be. "Interoffice Communications" from DOS came to me by the score.

He never bothered to telephone; he sent those communications, which had been dictated to his stenographer and were delivered by a fifth-assistant-director. One of these notices asked me to join a group to see Vivien Leigh model some costumes. The first one she wore was the one for the opening scene of GWTW, on the porch at Tara with the Tarleton twins. The dress was of fine white lawn with many lace-edged ruffles on the skirt that billowed over huge hoops; it had hundreds of little hand-sewn tucks and looked as if it had been weeks in the making instead of a few days. The green-eyed beauty who was to live in our hearts as Scarlett O'Hara looked lovely but the session was not devoted to Vivien's beauty nor the costumes. The talk centered on her bosom—or lack of it. Between sips of his Scotch-and-soda-and-no-ice, David Selznick grumbled that Vivien's bust was too small, that she had to have SEX if she attracted Rhett Butler, and he made it clear that SEX depended upon a large bosom; if she didn't have one, wardrobe should give her one. Wardrobe said they had fitted her with sponges but Selznick said she was still flat-chested and if Jean Harlow could look like she looked, howcome wardrobe couldn't fix Scarlett up.

The following day, an interoffice communication asked me to go to Leslie Howard's home for an accent lesson; the time was set for twelve, noon, and I was warned Mr. Howard did not like to be kept waiting. A veddy, veddy British maid met me at the door, asked me to "'ave a chair," and told me Mr. Howard was "talking on the trunk." I 'ad a chair and waited—and waited. At a quarter of one, he came downstairs, apologized for keeping me waiting, said he "bean talking on the trunk to London." He suggested it would be nice if I would stay for lunch and I accepted the invitation. The other guests included Vivien Leigh, Laurence Olivier, John Van Druten, John Balderston and Mr. Howard's secretary. British accents filled the room and I did not open my Southern mouth except to eat. When lunch was finished you'd have thought I was a Rhodes Scholar or, at least, a Cambridge graduate. I hurried back to the studio and telephoned some Macon friends so I could get the South back in my mouth.

Some months later came a communication asking me to go to a

certain hospital in Los Angeles to select a baby who would be filmed as the new-born Bonnie Blue Butler. By this time Mr. Selznick and I were good enough friends that I could sass him; I asked if he wanted me to pick out a baby who cried with a Southern accent.

Monty Westmore, head of makeup, showed me an interoffice communication "from DOS to Westmore" that informed Monty the child to be filmed as Melanie's son was supposed to be eleven months old in a certain scene. Later, the same child would be filmed in a scene in which he was eight months old. And would Mr. Westmore please see to it that the child was properly aged for each scene.

"You reckon he wants me to put a mustache on the eleven months old child?" Monty asked.

Along in June came a communication that informed me we'd shoot a scene tomorrow with Rhett Butler playing poker in jail, and it would not be necessary for me to teach a Southern accent to the Yankee guards.

Such questions as what sort of wedding ring Scarlett would have, how would she sign her name to the check used to pay off the taxes on Tara after the war, to what order did the nuns of Charleston, South Carolina, belong, would the girls take down their hair for the naps after the barbecue at Twelve Oaks, bothered me very little. But I was nonplussed when Vivien asked me how old Scarlett was at the end of the book. I said I'd check it out, I thought she was 26 or 28. She said:

"They want me to wear makeup in that last scene that will have bags under my eyes down to my navel. I won't do it. I am 28, and I don't look so damned old."

Though filming did not begin on that January morning as Mr. Selznick had decreed, it did begin the following Thursday. It went on, six days a week, often with three camera crews working on different scenes; and many a time we stayed on until midnight to finish filming and to see the "takes" of the day before. End of the job for me came in July, but retakes, changes in the musical scores, editing (two hours of film left on the cutting room floor), and making montage shots continued into late autumn. When the gala premiere was held December 15, 1939, the film barely got to Atlanta in time for the show.

When Mr. Selznick and GWTW's stars came to Atlanta for the premiere he told me he was worried that the characters in the movie did not sound exactly like the people he was meeting in Atlanta. I said:

"Never mind, David; this movie is so great nobody will notice if the characters speak Chinese."

There were times during the filming of GWTW when I was as bewildered as if Chinese had truly been the language of the movie. My confusion was caused by the frequent change in scripts. Time after time as I started home from the studio at night, somebody would hand me a new script; we'd shoot this tomorrow instead of the one we had been given two days ago for the scene. Though we had two complete scripts, all bound in handsome colors, one written by Sidney Howard, the other by Oliver H. P. Garrett, we got new scenes from day to day: Pink, yellow and blue pages indicating a rewriting of the original white pages.

During the process of filming the movie, various writers were called in to work on separate scenes, and Mr. Selznick, himself, wrote a lot of new scenes or versions of old ones. The writers I remember best: F. Scott Fitzgerald (he always wore dirty tennis shoes), Ben Hecht, Charles MacArthur (with whom I had little contact), John Balderston, and Sidney Howard.

Mr. Balderston invited me to come to his office for a consultation; he wanted to know what a Southern girl would say to the various beaux at the barbecue: "I'd know what to have an English girl say at the tea party, but a Southern girl at a barbecue!" He threw up his hands.

My advice was to let Scarlett say the same things to each of the men. A Southern girl doesn't get a new line for the old boyfriend; she gets a new boyfriend for the old line, I told him. "Just let Scarlett say to each one, something like 'I'm countin' on your eating barbecue with me, you handsome old thing, you." If you remember the scene at Twelve Oaks, you'll know Mr. Balderston took my advice.

Mr. Selznick wrote—or rewrote—many of the scenes, one of which was the cause of a sleepless night for me. One of his five or six secretaries phoned me at my apartment one evening to tell me Mr. Selznick had asked that I draw a plan of Aunt Pittypat's house in Atlanta that would help him in writing a scene that would take place in her home. He wants it, "tomorrow, please." What I knew about houseplans you could put in a half-closed eye of the fifth assistant director, but I sat up until early morning to draw some sort of plan. About ten o'clock that day, the secretary called to tell me Mr. Selznick had decided he did not need it.

When I heard the dialogue of the completed movie, I felt as if Margaret Mitchell had written much of it. Sidney Howard, who wrote the first script and got screen credit for it, told me that the writing was an easy job for him. "I took the dialogue straight out of the book," he said. Mr. Selznick must have done much the same when he wrote scenes, for he always spoke of the book in a sort of reverential tone, as if it were the Old Testament. When there was any question about any scene, the book was carefully searched to see just what Mitchell had written.

One day along in April of 1939, I had a memo from Mr. Selznick asking that I go to a certain office to meet Sidney Howard who was doing some new scenes and wanted to talk to me about one. I was excited at the prospect of meeting the eminent playwright and filled with wondering what the scene would be about; would he ask me about things I didn't know?

His office was huge and there were flowers on every table. He sat at one side of an enormous desk. I sat facing him. He thanked me for coming in, said Mr. Selznick wanted him to write a scene of Scarlett's second marriage, which would be held at the church with family and friends present for the ceremonies. Historian Wilbur Kurtz had assured Mr. Selznick that General Sherman did not put the torch to the Catholic Church in Atlanta, and the O'Hara family were Roman Catholics.

I was horrified! My reply was in a jumble of words: "You simply can't do it. A Hollywood church wedding will require lovely gowns for the ladies, dressed-up clothes for the men. Nobody has any decent clothes. We've shown Scarlett taking down the draperies in the parlor to make herself a dress to wear when she goes to see Rhett in jail. There's no money to use for buying any clothes if there were any available in Atlanta. The women haven't even got a pair of gloves that haven't been mended ten times. You just can't have a church wedding."

I stopped for breath and Mr. Howard came around the desk, bowed from the hips, took my hand and said, "Thank God somebody out here has some sense."

The church wedding scene was not filmed. Instead, to show that Scarlett had married Frank Kennedy, the screen displayed a large check in payment for the taxes on Tara; it was signed "Scarlett O'Hara Kennedy."

Mr. Howard and I became good friends, and we had some delightful chats about the idiosyncrasies of Movie Makers. He told me the story of his work on the script for GWTW: It goes like this:

In 1937, David O. Selznick phoned Sidney Howard in New York, offered him the script writing task, and urged him to come to Culver City for conferences and for the writing job. Howard agreed and a date was set for his arrival. He came, he phoned Mr. Selznick's office, he was told Mr. Selznick would see him tomorrow, to call back. The same thing happened the following day and again the next day, and the next. Howard waited three weeks at the hotel, never did see Mr. Selznick, so, still drawing his $1200.00 a week salary, he went back to New York where he worked on a play of his own. Some weeks later, Mr. Selznick telephoned Mr. Howard. "What the hell. Come on back out here at once." By this time Howard was at his farm in New England; he told Selznick, "I am just sitting down to dinner and have no idea of going anywhere at once." Then he hung up.

An hour or so later, Selznick phoned again; his urging of Howard finally brought his agreement to come out to Culver City in three weeks. He said he had three young heifers that would calve in two weeks and he couldn't leave them until all danger was past. Selznick probably had no idea what a heifer was, but he accepted Howard's word he'd come out in three weeks. He did and he stayed some six weeks, wrote the first draft of the script, and went back home, promising to return for cutting the length of the script when DOS called him to tell him how long he wanted the movie to play.

Some months later, Selznick phoned Howard he was coming to New York and wanted Howard to spend a few weeks working with him (Selznick) on editing the script. Howard, engaged in rehearsals for a Broadway play, demurred, finally agreed to work with Selznick each day from 9 a.m. until noon. Selznick arrived in New York with his retinue, took six suites at the Algonquin, phoned Howard, and they agreed to meet at the Selznick suite the next morning at nine. When Howard appeared he was told Selznick was asleep and had left word he was not to be disturbed. For three days, Howard returned to the Selznick suite each morning at nine, and found, each time, "Selznick was not to be disturbed." That was enough for Howard, who returned to his rehearsal duties, forgot GWTW until winter, when Selznick phoned once more: "Let's go together to Bermuda for a couple of weeks and cut the script." Howard said not on your life, his wife was about to have a baby and he had no notion of going anywhere and Selznick could go to hell and take the script with him.

Now, in April of 1939, Mr. Howard was in California, where he was doing some work for Metro-Goldwyn-Mayer; and David Selznick had successfully twisted the playwright's arm and spoken honeyed phrases in his ear, persuading him to come to an office at Culver City and do some new scenes for the movie. Whether the persuasion was helped along by Mr. Mayer who was Selznick's father-in-law, or whether there was a financial arrangement impossible to resist, Mr. Howard did not say. He did say, though, that Mr. Selznick was supposed to work with Howard, but the only time he'd seen DOS was on the set for a brief moment.

Due primarily to Margaret Mitchell's magnificent novel of the "Land of cavaliers and Cotton Fields called the Old South," and to David O. Selznick's faithful following of the book in his film, the people of the world remember how "in this Patrician world the Age of Chivalry took its last bow." As we salute Miss Mitchell and Mr. Selznick, let us also make a bow to Sidney Howard for his great script writing.

Georgia, April 1973

SETTING THE RECORD STRAIGHT

From Stephens Mitchell of Atlanta, only brother of Margaret Mitchell Marsh, came to me a letter about the column I had written about David Niven's book and its errors on facts about the life of the author of *Gone With the Wind*.

Mr. Mitchell wrote: "Thanks for your column in the *Macon Telegraph*. I appreciate the fact that you try to circulate the truth. However this is such an unheard of thing that you must be regarded as 'peculiar.'"

Mr. Mitchell sent me a copy of a letter which he had written to David Niven and sent to him in care of G. P. Putnam's Sons, publisher of *Bring on the Empty Horses*. Referring to Mr. Niven's statement that Miss Mitchell "died penniless," her brother wrote:

"This statement is not correct. Her 'trial balance' at the time of her death, according to her accountants, was $310,900.78. This did not include the value of royalty rights on her novel *Gone With the Wind*, nor did it include the value of motion picture rights nor the dramatic rights."

Mr. Mitchell also said of Mr. Niven's statement that "the earnings of *Gone With the Wind* came all in one year" is erroneous. "In fact, the book and the rights of it have produced a splendid income over the years. They still do. I paid over $30,000 in taxes on the income from this source for the year 1975.

"She did not complain of high taxation. She knew that if she did not like this country she was free to leave it at any time, and that while the purposes for which the taxes were levied might be silly or pointless, if a majority of our people were foolish, we must, in a democracy, submit until wise people were in the majority."

Referring to Mr. Niven's statement that Miss Mitchell was on the "knife edge of starvation for five years because she felt she had a great story to tell," Stephens Mitchell wrote:

"The facts were readily accessible in public records, or they could have been given by me, had you taken the trouble to ask me.

"If she had not had sufficient funds, her husband, who held a responsible position as head of the advertising department at Georgia Power Company, was a man of considerable means and made a good salary, which enabled them to live in a good section of the city— Ansley Park—and to enjoy themselves in any manner they saw fit.

"She was never on the knife edge of starvation. In addition to her husband's salary, she had a father, Eugene Mitchell, who was a man of means, and a brother, myself, who was well able to take care of her, had she been poor."

Referring to Mr. Niven's statement about the sale of the movie rights for the "measly sum of $50,000," Stephens Mitchell wrote:

"The motion picture rights were sold to the highest offerer. I, myself, conducted some of the negotiations for the sale. One large movie company offered $35,000 and the rest of the offers were at $25,000 or less."

The part of Mr. Mitchell's letter which appealed most of all to me came near the end: "The portion of your book about Margaret Mitchell Marsh seems to have been written without proper verification of the statements made in it. It is just pure folklore and not a true representation. I wish you had followed Mrs. Marsh's habit of long research, and fourfold verification of each statement of facts. The facts about the life of Margaret Mitchell Marsh can be gotten with ease. Just buy a copy of *Margaret Mitchell of Atlanta* by Finis Farr, published by William Morrow and Company in 1965.

"If these errors can get corrected in future editions of your book, Mrs. Marsh's family and her many friends will appreciate it."

Indeed they will, Stephens Mitchell.

Macon Telegraph, May 20, 1976

GWTW LETTERS REVEAL
THE REAL MARGARET MITCHELL

When *Gone With the Wind* was published in 1936, more than half of the reviewers of the book avowed they "sat up all night reading the book," that they "could not put it down." Now, forty years later, people are already saying they sat up all night reading *Margaret Mitchell's* Gone With the Wind *Letters, 1936-1949*, a book just two weeks old.

Published by Macmillan ($12.75), it is edited by Richard Harwell, curator of rare books and Georgiana at the University of Georgia. In his preface to the "Letters" Harwell tells us he has chosen the 427 letters from the more than 10,000 at the University with the hope that they reveal the personality of the remarkable young woman who wrote the novel that was translated in 27 languages, sold 21 million copies and has been read by an estimated 100 million people. He says: "I was free to range as widely as I wished in choosing which letters would most truly record Margaret Mitchell in what comes as close as anything ever will to being her biography."

I knew Margaret Mitchell rather intimately for 20 years, and I strongly approve of Harwell's selection. He has chosen wisely and well. The letters show her to be a woman of remarkable talent as a story teller; they show the difficulties that came with the publication of the book which the public took to its bosom and tried to take over her private life. The letters reveal her modesty, her desire for privacy, her wit and her charm.

Harwell tells us she told a *New York World Telegram* reporter that the two years of her life since publication had been "months of torment mixed with joy beyond comprehension," and this shows clearly in the letters.

Such a flood of letters and telegrams and telephone calls inundated her life that existence became almost unbearable. She wrote: "I hired another secretary and John and I and the two young ladies have been working as if we were shoveling coal." In 1936, *Time* magazine wired Miss Mitchell about GWTW and her husband, John Marsh, responded:

"Mrs. Marsh sick in bed as result of strain of becoming too famous." And that strain continued for years.

The list of persons to whom the letters went reads like a roster of America's great in the Thirties and Forties: Senator Walter George, Senator Richard Russell, Herschel Brickell, Virginius Dabney, Clifford Dowdey, Robert Sherwood, Ellen Glasgow, Vivien Leigh, David O. Selznick, Sidney Howard, and many, many more.

Among the "biographical" letters is one to Julia Collier Harris of the *Chattanooga Times*, in answer to a request from Mrs. Harris for information. The letter, dated April 28, 1936, was before the book's publication and before the flood of letters began coming to the author. Miss Mitchell writes, "I suppose I started in the cradle. Father is an authority on Atlanta and Georgia history of that period and Mother knew about as much as he did.... On Sunday afternoons when we went calling on the older generation of relatives, those who had been active in the Sixties, I sat on bony knees of veterans and fat slippery laps of great aunts and heard them talk about the times when Little Alex was visiting them...and how Grandpa Mitchell walked nearly fifty miles after Battle of Sharpsburg with his skull cracked in two places from a bullet."

That Miss Mitchell was "still fighting the war" is apparent in many letters that "took up for" the South. Typical is the letter she wrote Clifford Dowdey in reply to his letter about a piece he was writing for *The Southern Literary Messenger*," a piece to be titled "Are We Still Fighting the War?"

"As far as I can see," she wrote, "Appomattox didn't settle anything. We just got licked. Our situation, in spots, is much worse now than it was then and the problems are raising their heads once more. There is a good paragraph on this subject in Jonathan Daniel's 'A Southerner Discovers The South.' It's where he compares the South with Carthage and remarks that the Romans, after all, were politer than the Northern conquerors, for after they had sown Carthage with salt, they never rode through it on a railroad train and made snooty remarks about the degeneracy of the people who liked to live in such poor circumstances."

Her generosity and her "manners" are displayed in a letter to the Atlanta Chief of Police, thanking him for the "wonderful job" he and his men did during the festivities of the GWTW premiere, December 16, 1939. Though she had been besieged by visiting celebrities for the three days of the affair and had spent the previous evening seeing the first showing of the movie GWTW, making a speech from the stage, and giving a late-late party for the famous visitors, she found time the following day to thank the chief of police for his job well done.

Editor Harwell says it well in his introduction: "Success did not tarnish the charm of Margaret Mitchell... . Forty years after its publication Margaret Mitchell and her book are indelible parts of America. She furnished our past with a Scarlett O'Hara, a Melanie Wilkes, a Rhett Butler and an Ashley Wilkes. They are as American as Jefferson Davis and Robert E. Lee, Abraham Lincoln and Ulysses Grant, Tom Sawyer and Huckleberry Finn. Why, in a way they and the author belong to us all."

For millions of Americans, this collection of her letters will mean a better understanding of the greatness of the little woman who wrote such a big book.

Macon Telegraph, October 3, 1976

REVIEW ESSAY OF MARGARET MITCHELL'S GONE WITH THE WIND LETTERS

Margaret Mitchell's Gone With the Wind *Letters, 1936-1949.* Edited by Richard Harwell. (New York & London: Macmillan Publishing Co., Inc. 1976. Pp. xxxvi, 441. Illustrations, notes, & index. $12.95.)

Margaret Mitchell's Gone With the Wind *Letters* have joined with the letters written by the family and friends of Charles Colcock Jones to provide an important contribution to Georgia history. The Jones letters in *Children of Pride* were edited by Robert Manson Myers and published by Yale University Press in 1972; the Mitchell letters, edited by Richard Harwell, were published this fall by Macmillan. Miss Mitchell, as everybody knows, was an Atlanta native, the Reverend Mr. Jones was a native of Liberty County, and both Georgians wrote of life in the Sixties on a Georgia plantation, of the War Between the States, and of the "tragic era" of Reconstruction.

Harwell, author of many books on the Confederacy, is curator of rare books and Georgiana at the University of Georgia Library. He showed keen perception in his choice of the 427 letters which he selected from the more than 10,000 in the University Library, a gift of Stephens Mitchell, brother of Margaret. "I was freed to range as widely as I wished in choosing which letters would truly record Margaret Mitchell in what comes as close as anything ever will to being her biography," he wrote in his preface to the *Letters*. They provide a faithful picture of Margaret Mitchell and a history of the vicissitudes of a famous author. They also provide entertaining, amusing, delightful reading for us all.

In these letters is a history of the publication of a novel of the South and The War that sold 21 million copies, was translated into twenty-seven languages, and was read by an estimated 100 million people; a history of the making of a movie which has been the most popular one ever made and bids fair to go on forever; a history of the trials of an author who had become "too famous"; and in the letters is found the truth of what many of Miss Mitchell's friends said when they heard she was writing a book: "If she writes half as entertainingly as she talks, it will be a wonderful book." Mr. Harwell comments: "She did write as she talked, almost."

As a friend of Margaret Mitchell's who knew her before and after GWTW, I feel that I knew her better than most, and I found the *Letters* were so much like her that I felt, reading them, as if "Peggy Marsh" were spending the week-end with me and we were talking long into the night; or that I was once more in Hollywood (where everyone is slightly demented) reading a letter from her in answer to one I had written her about the wild goings-on in the movie world.

In one letter she wrote me during the filming of GWTW, she "was in stitches" over my report of a communication I had received from the costume director for the movie. He wanted my opinion on a note he had had from Producer Selznick which suggested that when the girls were taking their afternoon naps at Twelve Oaks on the day of the barbecue, their hoop skirts should be standing like sentinels along the walls of the room. She wrote me: "My congratulations to you for your success in the matter of dresses that were to defy the laws of gravity and stand up by themselves. I consider this a victory in the same category as the Miracle of the Marne."

In the midst of the confusion and the turmoil—telephones ringing at all hours, strangers popping into her home, people stopping her on the street to demand autographs, wild reports in newspapers that often caused her anguish in the misquoting—in all the trials that beset her after the publication of her book, as she strove to maintain her precious privacy, she wrote amusingly about it all. Harwell tells us she told a New York *World-Telegram* reporter that the two years of her life since publication had been "months of torment mixed with joy beyond comprehension." When *Time* magazine telegraphed her about a statement in the book, her husband, John Marsh, wired: "Mrs. Marsh sick as a result of strain of becoming too famous." The strain continued the rest of her life but she never lost her marvelous ability to write about it with humor. When the flood of letters and telegrams and telephone calls inundated her life so that existence was almost unbearable, she wrote: "I hired another secretary and John and I and the two young ladies have been working as if we were shoveling coal."

To Herschel Brickell in 1938 she wrote: "Writing books aint no pleasure, and ditch digging is a far easier profession." To a correspondent in Germany who had said in a letter to her that he had told his friends she had not written another book, she wrote: "I have had no leisure in which to do any writing at all, as the success of my book has brought a multitude of problems of both business and personal nature, so that I scarcely have time to buy myself some winter clothes...young Southern girls, by the hundreds, have been after me for the last two years pleading with me to endorse them for this part (Scarlett's). I have nothing to do with the film and cannot be of any assistance to them. Nevertheless, these young ladies have taken up two years of my time with their importunities."

Particularly revealing of Miss Mitchell's Southern background is a letter to Julia Collier (Harris) of the Chattanooga Times. Miss Mitchell wrote Mrs. Harris of her ancestry and her Atlanta girlhood, of how she learned to "recite" on Friday afternoons at school and her pieces, picked by her father and mother, were Henry Grady's "The New South," "Little Giffen of Tennessee," and "The Conquered Banner." (See Appendix IV.) She wrote: "As to how I got started on Civil War material, I suppose I started in the cradle. Father is an authority on Atlanta and Georgia history of that period and Mother knew about as much as he did. I heard so much, when I was little, about the fighting and the hard times after the war that I firmly believed Mother and Father had been through it all instead of being born long afterward. On Sunday afternoons when we went calling on the older generation of relatives, those who had been active in the Sixties, I sat on bony knees of veterans and slippery laps of great aunts and heard them talk about the times when 'Little Alec' was visiting them... . and how Grandpa Mitchell walked nearly fifty miles after the battle of Sharpsburg with his skull cracked in two places by a bullet."

Miss Mitchell's passionate love of the South and her zealous defense of her native land show up in many of her letters: there's one to Clifford Dowdey in reply to his that told her he was writing a piece for the Southern Literary Messenger and planned to title it "Are We Still Fighting The War?" She told him she had a good laugh at his title, and added: "As far as I can see, Appomattox didn't settle anything. We just got licked. Our situation in spots is much worse now than it was then and problems are raising their heads once more. There is a good paragraph on this subject in Jonathan Daniels' 'A Southerner Discovers the South.' It's where he compares the South with Carthage and remarks that the Romans, after all, were politer than the Northern conquerors, for after they had sown Carthage with salt, they never rode through it on a railroad train and made snooty remarks about the degeneracy of the people who liked to live in such poor circumstances."

She writes, too, in another letter (to Louis Harris of the *Augusta Chronicle*): "I recall one time when *Time* magazine with its usual anti-Southern bias was so ill advised as to query me on an item in *Gone With the Wind* about the looting of Atlanta cemeteries by Federal soldiers, the stealing of wedding rings from dead fingers and the wrenching of silver name plates from coffins. I had four or five references, myself. I thought dealing with people like *Time* it was better to have more and I spoke to some of my reference library friends and they aroused sister librarians. They are a combination of blood hound, ferret and angel, and they aroused sister librarians all over the South and for nearly six months eye witness accounts of the depredations of the Union soldiers in Southern cemeteries kept coming in. Of course *Time* was very careful not to print any of them except in something they called a supplement of letters which no one ever saw."

That Miss Mitchell was not planning to write any more books, despite the thousands of rumors to the contrary, is repeated in many of her letters. To Producer Selznick, replying in 1939 to his request that she write some script for the movie, she explained some of her reasons why no more books: "For nearly three years I have had no time for writing of any kind. With hundreds of letters coming in, with the telephone ringing, with people clamoring for 'an introduction to Mr. Selznick' and the newspapers bedeviling me for a statement on subjects which do not concern me, I have had no time even to think about creative writing, much less attempt it." To another correspondent she wrote: "It was good for you to write that you were waiting to read some more books written by me. I, too, would like to read some more books written by me. . . . Since 1936 I've been a business woman and a nurse rather than a writer, for handling business matters concerning GWTW in this country and in almost every civilized European country is a full time job." She told her correspondent of the five-year illness of her father and of the recent illness of her husband and how they had kept her busy as a nurse.

It has been often said of Margaret Mitchell that she was a "Scarlett," but many considered her more the Melanie type. In truth, she had characteristics of both of her heroines and her letters bear this out. There is a Melanie letter written to the Atlanta Chief of Police, thanking him and his men for the "wonderful job" they did during the festivities of the GWTW premiere in December 1939. Though she had been besieged by visiting celebrities for the three days of the festivities and had spent the evening of the premiere viewing the first showing of the film, making a speech from the stage after the show, and giving a late-late party for the stars, she found time and energy the next morning to write a thank-you note. Margaret Mitchell had "manners"; she was always considerate of others. Then there is the letter to Producer Selznick's assistant, Miss Rabwin, in which the author showed that she could sneak in the stiletto even as Scarlett might have done, and been "mannerly" all the while. She wrote to Miss Rabwin about some stills of the movie stars which she had mailed to Miss Mitchell:

"You note that these pictures are for my private use and you requested that I keep them from 'prying eyes of the news-hawks.' Of course I will do this, and any other pictures or communications which may come to me from you or Mr. Selznick will be held confidential. I write you this so that you will not think I betrayed your confidence and gave to the newspapers the pictures which appeared yesterday and which I am enclosing. They are from the morning paper." The pictures were identical with those which Miss Rabwin had sent.

Mr. Harwell wrote that Miss Mitchell "never let success go to her head." The letter she wrote to the secretary of the Board of Trustees at Smith College when the institution was about to confer a degree upon her is an indication of her modesty. She wrote that she had never received a degree, either conferred or otherwise, and she would be grateful if the secretary would write her all the particulars so that Miss Mitchell would do the proper thing. The secretary wrote her that reservations would be made for her at the hotel and when she arrived her cap and gown would be at the hotel and that all directions would be given her upon arrival. The secretary asked that Miss Mitchell write her the correct head size for the cap and size for the gown. But she failed to ask how tall the author was (only four feet, eleven inches.) So, Miss Mitchell found when she tried on the gown that it "trailed for yards" on the floor and the sleeves "dragged the ground."

Did she telephone the secretary and complain? Not Margaret

Mitchell. She telephoned the hotel housekeeper and borrowed a needle and a spool of black cotton thread and spent the late hours of the evening shortening the sleeves and the gown. She almost burst with laughter as she told of the incident on her return to Georgia. And she found it amusing, though a bit embarrassing, when somebody told her she was wearing the tassel of her cap on the wrong side of her head.

Truly Margaret Mitchell is as much a part of Georgia history as Mr. Harwell indicated in his introduction to the *Letters*: "Success did not tarnish the charm of Margaret Mitchell. Forty years after its publication Margaret Mitchell and her book are indelible parts of America." She is also as much a part of Georgia history as James Edward Oglethorpe or 'Little Alec' Stephens or Abraham Baldwin or Jimmy Carter.

_____

Georgia Historical Quarterly, Winter 1976, pp. 372-378

SPEECH
DUBLIN, GEORGIA

We do not know her audience. A draft of the talk, with penciled notes, was in her papers. She told some events so often that she gave herself only a cue for the story. These cues are given in **bold, italic type.**

Few of you in this room are old enough to remember that I visited my Uncle Cincy and Aunt Kate here back in the twenties and thirties. But I had two uncles who lived here and my sister, Allie Myrick, taught the sixth grade (I THINK it was the sixth, anyway she taught here). So, I have fond memories of this town and I am especially pleased to be invited to speak to you all.

I had known for two years that I might go to Hollywood when the shooting of GWTW began and I had almost given up the idea when the word came. As with all Hollywood doings the word came in a strange fashion. The man called long distance and wanted to know if I could come tomorrow. I said not that soon. I had a job and I had to arrange to leave and I had to pack up a few things and arrange about subleasing my apt. and so on. So, he said Oh, come as soon as possible and was I afraid to fly.

No, I wasn't. So they arranged for my ticket to be charged to the Studio and I could get the reservation to suit my convenience. But please call collect as to time of arrival.

When I got there, I found nobody was waiting for filming to start. We had a meeting—everybody who was to manage things met; no actors. There were costume designers, set designers, script writers, hairdressers, makeup people, grips, electricians, somebody in charge of "don't spend so much money," and the Director George Cukor.

Were the costumes ready? The costume man asked how could he get costumes ready when the actors hadn't been decided upon. He had been waiting to get measurements for a month.

Somebody said okay get the measurements for those people, and the costume man said he couldn't make dresses by measurement, he had to put clothes on people.

Mr. Cukor said we would start shooting on the 16th—the meeting was on the 13th—and the costume man said he would make costumes if he had some actors to fit them on, and Mr. Cukor said where is Gable and somebody said they had been trying to get in touch with him for ten days and Cukor said well get in touch with him right away because we'd start shooting on the 16[th.] The assistant director said we might shoot something on the 16th, but there wouldn't be anything to shoot the next day. Somebody said what about Mammy, had she been selected yet, and somebody else said why not get Marian Anderson the black opera star for Mammy. Nobody bothered to answer THAT.

Arguments and orders continued for two hours, and as far as I could see when the meeting broke up nobody had done anything, but we were supposed to start shooting in three days.

But I go back now to my arrival in Hollywood—as we call the mad, zany part of Los Angeles that is the movie world. Actually the Selznick Studios were in Culver City, about a 30-minute ride from Hollywood itself. The contract I had gotten by telegram was six typed pages long and said in effect that I was to stay for six weeks as technical adviser on accents of the white actors, dialects of the Blacks, and on customs and manners of the Old South. Well, I knew pretty well about Negro dialect of the 1860s. I was brought up with it all around me. My father ran a 1500-acre plantation that was owned from five generations back and the Negroes on the place were children or grandchildren or great grandchildren of former slaves. The place was run much like Be Fo De Wah. Some people call that late trouble of the Sixties a Civil War, others War Between the States, but the dyed in the wool Southerner of my generation dubbed it "De Wah" and everybody wished many a time for things to be as they were Be Fo De Wah. So, as I said, our place was run much like Be Fo De Wah.

Unker Taylor Dawson made baskets. Unker Tom was the well digger and cleaner outer. About fifteen families lived on the place and each family had a well. Most of them had a spring, too. But it kept Unker Tom busy cleaning out wells and digging new ones when an old one ran dry. The blacksmith was Unker Jack and he had a forge and a shop and shod the mules and mended buggy wheel rims and sharpened plows.

We had so many mules I never knew their names, except Annie and Lou were the ones in our home stable, used for cutting grass and tending the small acreage that Papa kept going for the family. A man named Sherman was the yard man and house man, and ate his meals in the kitchen after we had ours, and in the evenings he sat by the kitchen stove and told tales to us, the chillum in the Myrick household.

Brer Rabbit, etc.

So, as you can see I knew about the colored folks, as we were taught then to call what we now must call Blacks.

I also knew about the manners of the Southern lady. My grandma had taught me by the time I was 13 that a lady never crossed her legs. She could cross her ankles but not her legs at the knee.

A lady rode forward in the buggy and the man faced her. If she let him sit beside her she was considered fast.

I knew many things that I never dreamed anybody would ask me. For instance, one of the first things they asked me at Culver City was what kind of head rag Mammy would wear and how it would be tied. They asked me what sort of wedding ring Scarlett would wear. They asked me how she would sign her name to a check. She married Frank Kennedy after her first husband died so she could use his money to save Tara as the taxes were about to get it. And to show she had paid the Tara taxes, the movie wanted to show a check for the amount drawn by Scarlett in her new name. She signed it Scarlett O'Hara Kennedy. I never have known to this day whether I was right or not.

But the main problem I faced was the accent of the white folks in the movie. Southern accent, my contract said. But there is not really any such thing as THE Southern accent. There are easily five different ones in the State of Georgia. People in Savannah and Brunswick do not have the same accent as we have in Macon or you have in Dublin. And people in Atlanta and Clayton County don't have the same sort of speech as we have and you have. The mountain folks of Georgia have a distinctive speech of their own.

And the good lawd knows none of us really talk the way the Yankees think we talk. I knew from the awful garble of the Southern speech I'd heard on radio programs that the Yankees had a strange idea of our speech. And I knew if Scarlett O'Hara said in GWTW something like "Ahm go tho my arms rat roun yall's nake," the Southerners would fire on Fort Sumter again.

After I had argued with Mr. Selznick for about a week we agreed to have the people in GWTW speak the sort of speech people are accustomed to hear on stage and screen, we'd pronounce R like AH.

"Are you?" No. "Ah you?"

Another thing fairly common to Georgians is to pronounce a short O differently from the Yankee way. We say "own" for "on," and we don't say "dog" we say "dawg." We don't drink "coffee" but "cawfee." And we are likely to drink our likkeh straight.

Reminds me of mint julep on the set... Get em while dey hot.

We agreed the actors would speak good stage English with no Rs and would pronounce certain words in what is the Georgia way of speaking, not to try to teach Gable to sound like Charleston and Ashley Wilkes to speak like a Virginian. And we'd give the feeling of the South with Southern idiom. The book was full of it—Miss Mitchell was marvelous with Southern speech words. "Like a duck on a June bug" and "Miss Scarlett, you come in de house. I ain't gone have you gittin your back all sun burned after I cleared up your skin wid butte milk when you been to Savannah." That decided, all I had to do was work with them all trying to get them to sound sufficiently Southern to please everybody in Georgia, Alabama, Mississippi, Louisiana, and so on.

I had my troubles. Confidentially I have a very bad habit of mimicking the speech of the people around me. I go to New York City and in a few hours talk like I was born there. Well, I had one hilarious time about Leslie Howard, a Britisher who didn't want to bother to give up his British accent.

Quote The snow is deep in Virginia etc.

I got a note one day to get a car and go to Mr. Howard's house and spend an hour with him discussing a scene.

Story of me going British.

Miss Leigh, also British, was easy to work with and wanted to be the perfect Scarlett and to please the South in everything. She even tried to make her eyes look as green as possible when Southern visitors were on the set where the shooting was going on.

Love and Mother story

Gable still had some Western sounds in his voice. But he had been on screen and had had speech lessons and there was not much to bother about. He still said R not AH.

Can't afford a four door Ford.

Now Mammy and Prissy. Mostly what I did for six months of shooting the film was sit on the set and listen to the accents, and if they went wrong to say so to the director. He'd call, "OK for me. OK for the camera. OK for Dixie?"

But I still had my troubles. Selznick wrote notes. "Please get car to central hospital select a baby to be photographed as Bonnie Blue—child of Rhett." I wrote back ok but did he expect me to select baby who cried with a Southern accent.

Cotton chopping story.

Oh everybody was a little nutty on the Selznick lot. They asked me shortly after I arrived if we had nice clouds in Georgia. I was a little puzzled but finally made out they wanted to know if we had big white thunderheads that photographed nicely. I said nobody—not even California—could have better clouds than Georgia. Now that was in early February, but it was not until late May that they got around to photographing the outdoor scenes where Gerald O'Hara rides over his plantation the late afternoon before the barbecue at Twelve Oaks. We could not shoot in the area of Los Angeles—too many eucalyptus trees, pepper trees and Jacaranda trees and no big oaks or hickories or chinaberries or dogwoods or persimmons or poplars in Los Angeles. So they brought me pictures of an area about 200 miles north with big oaks and sloping hillsides and nice branches or creeks that could get by with looking like north Georgia. The town, Chico, was not far from the capital at Sacramento.

By the time the crew got to Chico it had reached the dry season in California—sometimes no rain for weeks and weeks and nary a cloud was to be seen. We played poker and read books and sat around in the shade and talked for five days before a picture was made. That is I did. The poor men who had to get things ready worked. The grass had all turned brown. The hired help went over acres of grass and sprayed them with green paint so the grass looked like springtime. Remember, the barbecue was on the 15th of April. Other helpers had tied thousands of pink paper flowers on small trees to give the effect of apple blossoms in a long shot. We called the painting director Mayfield Parrish, a popular print maker of the early twenties.

After five days, clouds formed and shooting began. The weather was a most important part of the shooting schedule. I remember when we got the advance sheets, telling us what would be the shooting schedule for tomorrow—going to the barbecue at Twelve Oaks. Gerald O'Hara would ride in a carriage with the two younger daughters, Ellen and Scarlett in a second carriage, the Tarleton twins and half a dozen other young men on horseback, the parents of the Tarleton twins in a carriage etc. There would be no talk recorded, but I was to be there to observe if I thought anything might not be Southern custom! And be there at 9 a.m. which was better than the usual schedule "be there at seven." Well, I was at the back lot, known as Forty Acres, at a quarter to nine, but the fog was so thick I could scarcely see the guard at the gate. The horses and carriages were all on hand, the director and his assistants were milling about among light men and grips and hairdressers and so on. The first assistant director, a delightful Britisher (Eric Stacey), had a pact with himself; he would not tie his shoes until the first take of the day had been made.

Well, that day he didn't tie his shoes off at all. The fog refused to lift. Nobody but me bothered about the expense of the day, but to my overly stricken viewpoint, it was awful how much the day was costing and nothing done. A carriage and pair of horses with driver cost $500 a day. Each horse and saddle and bridle cost $150 a day. The handlers of the horses cost $50 a day, just to hold the horses until the riders got aboard. Well, I figured the cost of the day's equipment was about $6,000. Not to mention the salaries of all those people, including me, who just sat around and killed time. Of course, that was 1939. The cost today would run into many times that figure.

The worst spell of weather came when we were shooting the scene where Scarlett eats that radish, retches and says she'll never be hungry again. The scene was to be shot at something called Lasky Mesa, a desolate place about 50 miles from the Culver City studio, and it was to be made at sunrise. We had to meet at the Selznick lot at 3 a.m.

Again fog had taken over most of Southern California, but we got into buses and started for the Mesa about 3:30 a.m. I could only be glad I was not driving the bus. It was darker than a moonless night in a forest. We got to the Mesa all right, about 5 a.m. The sun was to rise at 6 and the men got busy setting things up, though they grumbled to each other that the damned fog would never lift before sunrise. Sho nuff, it didn't. About the time the sun should have been rising, the director said take a break for breakfast and a box lunch was served and that hot coffee helped cut down our shivers. It was cold as well as foggy. We crowded into the buses and went back to the studio. No more work today, we could go home and catch up on sleep. We'd shoot tomorrow at the Mesa. Meet in Culver City at 3 a.m.

This went on for three days. On the fourth day, all went well and

Scarlett retched in admirable style and the first take was perfect. We had another day off.

On holidays we got paid time and a half, so the crowd was delighted to work May 30, Memorial Day. One of the cast said to me, "How do you like working on Memorial Day?" I laughed. "This isn't really Memorial Day in the South, and this is a Southern picture so it doesn't matter. April 26 is really Memorial Day for the Confederacy." We were shooting the scene where Mammy goes upstairs with Melanie at Scarlett's house. Rhett is locked in the room with Bonnie's dead body, after she was killed from being thrown from her jumping pony. You may remember: Mammy went to the door to meet Melanie who had come to express her sorrow. The two climbed the stairs together at Rhett's house and Mammy, crying the while, said, "Miss Mellie, I don't know what we gwine do. Mr. Rhett ain't gwine let us bury dat chile." We shot THAT one for ten hours on May 30 and again for eight hours the next day. Mammy blowing lines, the mike in picture, camera troubles, lighting wrong—all sorts of technicalities. That scene was another one of my minor troubles. The prop man had asked me about the funeral wreath on the front door at Rhett's house, for there was to be a shot of the front door to show that death was in the family. I told props to get a small bouquet of white roses with white ribbons for the door. They sent for me to come see it for approval. "Lawdy, Mis Scarlett, the roses in California grow as big as green cabbages in a Georgia field." The bouquet would have been big enough for the funeral of the Shah of Iran! I asked the man to find some small roses or rose buds and cut the decoration size by more than half. They finally ended up with artificial roses—and a long shot so nobody could tell.

How did I get the job?
How did I like the actors? Gable good ole boy.
Vivien bright, anxious to please, green eyes, temper, director fight.
Mellie like her name, gentle and sweet.
Mammy marvelous.

Prissy, well I'll tell you. The best scene in the show is the one where Prissy goes to tell Cap'n Butler Miss Mellie done had her baby. You remember she had told Miss Scarlett she didn't know nothing about birthin' babies. "Ma never would let me stay round when folks was havin' em. She wear me out wid a bresh broom." And I feel about the movie just as Prissy felt about that baby when she told Cap'n Butler, "Me and Miss Scarlett brought dat baby but hit was mostly me."

November 18, 1976

A WITNESS RECALLS FILMING OF GWTW

Review of *Scarlett, Rhett and a Cast of Thousands*

I spent six months in California as technical adviser for the movie *Gone With the Wind*, on accent, manners and customs of the Old South—on the lot at Culver City, known as the Forty Acres, where we shot the greater portion of the movie; out at Lasky Mesa where we made the scene in which Scarlett retches after eating a radish and says she will never be hungry again; in Chico, where we made the shots of Gerald O'Hara riding over his plantation meeting his daughter and telling her that at the barbecue tomorrow at Twelve Oaks Mellie's engagement to Ashley Wilkes would be announced; in the MGM lot where we made the shot of Bonnie falling to her death as she jumped her pony over the obstructions; and in various places where we made shots of Belle Watling, Aunt Pittypat's house, the ride of Scarlett and Rhett out of the burning Atlanta, and others. I spent 12 to 15 hours a day with the shooting crews, the various directors and the script girls who were making the famous movie. But there was a lot about the movie production I didn't know.

So, I got a lot of information when I read Roland Flamini's book *Scarlett, Rhett and a Cast of Thousands*, newly published by Macmillan. I knew it took so long to make the movie that finances were low and Jock Whitney caused many whispers behind hands when he visited the set ("I expect Mr. Selznick will be on the set early tomorrow, Mr. Whitney is in town"), but I never knew Mr. Selznick was broke when the movie was only about half finished. That is, I never knew it until I read Flamini's book. I knew Vivien Leigh had a temper and that it flared often when she and director Fleming disagreed on how Scarlett would act, but until I read Flamini's book I never knew Vivien used four-letter words.

Some of the things Flamini tells are twice-told tales, and some of them are not relevant to the movie's making, it seems to me. There are many little stories of such things as bawdy toys and dirty jokes without which the book would have been improved.

But despite digression from the actual movie making the book has much that the public will want to read. Flamini has done a fine job on research, gathering facts and quotes from myriad sources; he writes feelingly and entertainingly in a fashion you expect from a *Time* magazine correspondent.

Naturally, the first thing I did when I got my hands on the book was turn to the index and see how many times (if at all) "Susan Myrick" was noted. I had read with a mixture of ego and blushes the review that Don Floyd wrote for the *Telegraph*, last Sunday, and I was greatly pleased to be given such a generous spot in his review. I agree with Don that Flamini "might have done better." But there's no doubt in my mind that everybody will buy the book and talk about it for months to come.

There are scores of pictures in the book, many of them familiar to us who have been reading about GWTW for years, but many of them new and all of them interesting.

And there are wonderful bits: How Mr. Selznick "fired" director Cukor and cameraman Lee Garmes and publicity man Russell Birdwell; what a magnificent job Bill Menzies did as art director for the production; how there were 27 copies of the print dress Scarlett wore in about one third of the movie, the copies in gradual stages of disintegration "that seemed to mirror the collapse of the South"; of how many, many scenes for the movie were written only to be discarded and have a substitute made; and a description of cutting and editing the film that is a great piece of writing.

Flamini considers Selznick a genius of sorts as well as a man who is hard to get along with and full of ego. He gives credit to the producer for the magnificence of many scenes of the movie. Says he:

"In the end, *Gone With the Wind* remained a picture with a war setting and no battle scenes. War is seen with its destructive effect on people and places, never in its panoply and excitement. The 'spectacle' in *Gone With the Wind* consists of scenes of death without glory like the railway depot sequence, culminating in the famous traveling crane shot of Confederate wounded and dying."

Mr. Flamini, however, fails to give some of the credit to Margaret

Mitchell's book. It is a story of the war's "destructive effect on people and places," not "its panoply and excitement."

A story seldom told is Flamini's carefully researched one of the profits derived from the movie. Selznick is quoted as saying, "Everything in *Gone With the Wind* is, without exception, as I wanted it to be. I took a gamble on my own conceptions and my own methods." But the gamble paid off more handsomely for others than for Selznick. In the end, the lion's share went to Metro. By 1967 the movie had earned $75 million for Metro. It will undoubtedly go on earning money for years to come.

But David Selznick was right when he said (according to Flamini): "When I go they'll put on my tombstone, 'Here lies the man who made *Gone With the Wind.*'"

Macon Telegraph, February 5, 1976

RICHARD BARKSDALE HARWELL

Sue's Introduction of Harwell to the Macon Writers Club at its Annual Breakfast, April 2, 1977

Two score years ago, plus a few days, a petite young woman with Titian hair, a square jaw, a pointed chin and a fascinating personality was the guest of honor and the speaker at the Annual Breakfast of the Macon Writers Club. The following day, Miss Blythe McKay reported in the *Macon Telegraph*'s Woman's section (I quote)

"Miss Mitchell enchanted the more than 200 guests with her informality and her subtle humor. She said she came to the breakfast thrice handicapped. First, she was substituting for Edison Marshall who was to have been honor guest; second, she had attended a breakfast the club had given for Helen Topping Miller and had heard Mrs. Miller's impressive talk on the trend of literature, and she, herself, wouldn't know a literary trend if it came up and bit her; and third, she was not really an author yet, she wouldn't be published for three weeks and one can't be an author until she is published."

Miss Margaret Mitchell became an author, officially, when GWTW was published in June, 1936 and before Christmas, a million copies of the famous novel had been sold. The following year, Miss Mitchell was awarded the Pulitzer Prize.

It is therefore, as Mammy would say, "fitten" that our speaker today is a man who probably knew Miss Mitchell better than most. As editor of Margaret Mitchell's GWTW Letters, he read some 10,000 of the author's letters to various persons, and selected from them 427 which he included in the book. He said, "In selecting these, I was privileged to range as widely as I wished in choosing which letters would most thoroughly and most truly record Margaret Mitchell in what would come as near as anything ever will to being her autobiography." Those who knew Peggy Marsh best join in high praise for Mr. Harwell's wise selections.

Our speaker says that he never knew Margaret Mitchell until in the spring of 1936 — that eventful spring which brought forth the publication of GWTW. "I first met Peggy when I attended the Atlanta Library Club meeting at which she told the fertilizer story she wrote out in a letter to Harold Latham. I sat by her that evening, and we were never introduced as, when we saw one another, we realized we had been speaking for years at the Carnegie Library and in the environs of Ansley Park. She and John were on my brother's paper route (*The Georgian*) and I used to deliver their paper occasionally when I substituted for my brother.

"I saw her only a few times until I had several meetings with her during the bond sales for the cruiser *Atlanta*, but I did not really get to know her until after World War II. I saw her fairly frequently in the last two years of her life. As far as I know, my (book) *Confederate Music* was the only book by one of her friends that she ever read in manuscript, and it was at her request, not mine. That book was published by the University of North Carolina Press in 1950 and is dedicated to her."

Born in Washington, Wilkes County, birthplace of many other prominent Georgians, he earned his AB in English at Emory University, his ABLS at the Library School of the University, and Doctorate of Literature at New England College. Before "The Letters" were published, he was probably best known for his one-volume abridgements of Douglas Southall Freeman's biographies of Lee and Washington. He is author and editor of more than two score other books, most of them about the American War Between the States or about American Literary figures.

He has served as Librarian of Bowdoin, Smith and Georgia Southern Colleges. He is at present curator of Rare Books and Georgiana at the University of Georgia Library.

If I should list for you all the articles he has published he would have no time left in which to make a speech. But I cannot forebear to mention a book he wrote, published by the Bee Hive Press at Savannah, called *The Mint Julep*.

Our speaker is probably the only man in Georgia who knows that the English poet John Milton wrote a tribute to the Julep in 1673.

In his opening paragraph he writes, "Wherever there is a mint julep there is a bit of the Old South. For the julep is part ceremony, tradition, and regional nostalgia; part flavor, taste and aroma and only by definition liquor, simple syrup, mint and ice. It is all delight. It is nectar to the Virginian, mother's milk to the Kentuckian, and ambrosia to Southerners everywhere."

Today he comes as our speaker, a worthy follower of the many literary figures who have been Writers Club speakers over the years. Ladies and gentlemen, I present Richard Barksdale Harwell.

Editor's Note: In Sue's handwriting at bottom of first page, **Peggy at writers club, Mar. 1936.**

MARGARET MITCHELL
JOINS HALL OF FAME

Margaret Mitchell was posthumously inducted into the Georgia Press Institute's Hall of Fame at the Henry W. Grady School of Journalism and Mass Communications at a luncheon meeting on February 24 in Athens. At that meeting, Richard Harwell, curator of rare books at the University of Georgia libraries, as a representative of the Mitchell family, delivered a brief biographical essay about her great interest in the Georgia Press Institute.

"Margaret Mitchell was by no means prideful, but she was proud indeed of a few things: Of her family, of *Gone With the Wind*, of being a working newspaper woman, and of her participation with her friends in the meetings of the Georgia Press Association and the annual Press Institute," he said.

Mr. Harwell has graciously given me permission to quote from his speech. He said that "for this group a biography of her is superfluous. Many of you knew her better than I did.... . I say merely that she was born in Atlanta, November 8, 1900—at 296 Cain Street which has now, unfortunately, disappeared, as she would doubtless be embarrassed at having to say she was born in a home on International Boulevard. She worked on the *Atlanta Journal* Sunday magazine section from late 1922 until mid 1926. In 1925 she married another veteran of the Atlanta city room, John R. Marsh.

"...Fame burst upon her when her book, *Gone With the Wind*, was published in 1936. From then till her untimely death in 1949 she was a prisoner of her own fame, steadfastly determined to keep her private life while bearing her public life as an author and as Georgia's best known citizen, like the great lady that she was."

Miss Mitchell's love for the newspaper folks of the Georgia press was set down in a letter which she wrote to Herschel Brickell in 1938. Mr. Harwell quoted from the letter: "There's no news in particular, which in my case means good news. It is due to this happy state of affairs that we are going to the editor's convention. Of course, the Georgia press has been wonderful to me since the beginning, not only in their reviews and kind remarks but in their sheltering attitude, which has gone far toward making life endurable. Two years ago when I went to one of their conventions the president arose in open meeting and declared that none of them wanted my old autograph and none of them thought a bit more of me than they did before. Such an attitude has made it possible for me to live in Georgia and jaunt about the state with the freedom I formerly enjoyed. Now that the wind has blown over I am certainly grateful to all Georgia editors for what they did for me."

That the Press Institute was especially dear to Miss Mitchell is shown in a column written by Bob Considine in his syndicated column in 1949, Harwell said, and he quoted from that column:

"Every once in a while someone comes up with a story that Margaret Mitchell, whose *Gone With the Wind* saved 149,718 novelists from continuing to try to write the great American novel, is writing another book. Saw her last week at her favorite convention, that of the Georgia Press Institute. Regret to say she is not writing another novel, nor any thing else. Her concern remains the complete recovery of her former newspaperman husband, John Marsh."

In the letters of Margaret Mitchell are many wonderful memories of the Press Institute, Harwell said, and who could know better than he who read some 12,000 letters in his job of selecting about 450 of them for publication in the book *Margaret Mitchell's* Gone With the Wind *Letters*.

And in the memories of the editors who meet annually for the Georgia Press Institute are many recollections of the delight of a conversation with "Peggy Marsh" at the conventions.

———————————

Macon Telegraph, March 30, 1978

This is the last item we know of that Sue wrote about GWTW or her friend Peggy. She did, however, appear in a TV program about the movie that aired on an Atlanta station the night that GWTW was first shown on TV. Her interview on a DVD is available from the editor. See the end pages for more information.

AFTEREFFECTS OF THE WAR
BETWEEN THE STATES

Every Southern family was affected by The War. This segment is three stories Susan Myrick wrote for the *Macon Telegraph* in the early 1930s and explores how three families fared during and after The War.

Susan interviewed the soldier in the first article only a short time before his death. He was the last Confederate veteran living in Milledgeville, Susan's home town.

The matriarch of the family on Pio Nono Avenue in Macon was a slave; the Jackson sisters ran a 600-acre farm after the war, with no men to help. Susan could not have picked a better trio of subjects to show how the war affected the survivors.

A SOLDIER'S TALE

Algernon Sidney Tennille was born November 27, 1842 and died May 25, 1931, shortly after this interview with Susan Myrick.

"The thin gray line" has grown heart-breakingly thin. Few of the men who fought in the War Between the States are alive and fewer still are those who took up arms at the beginning of the war and fought all the way through. But Milledgeville boasts a veteran 89 years old, who volunteered when the first call came and carried on through four weary years of hopeless endeavor. He is A. S. Tennille, known to the employees of the state hospital for the insane where he has worked for 47 years, as "Uncle Polk," having received the nickname as a small boy when his father voted for Polk when he ran against Clay for president.

Mr. Tennille counts as the most important event of the war, the time he saw and talked to General Robert E. Lee, Commander-in-Chief of the Army. More to be remembered than the day he was shot at Cold Harbor, or the time he received the bullet wound at Seven Pines, or the exchange of tobacco for coffee with the soldiers from the other side, or the time he swiped the potatoes from the hill which was closely guarded.

"What did General Lee talk to you about?" I asked him.

"About making syrup."

"Making syrup! Why on earth would the Commander of the Confederate Armies talk to you about making syrup?"

A smile stole over his gentle old face. He sat in an easy chair on the front porch of his daughter's home, his walking stick lying across his knees and his blue eyes twinkling.

"I'll tell you how it was. There was an old man who had a cane patch near the place we were encamped in Virginia and the soldiers were stealing his cane. So he appealed to the Major to send him a guard for his cane patch. I was one of the men detailed to guard that cane. I saw he had an old mule out in his yard and a cane mill, so I told him I knew how to make syrup and would make it for him if he would let me and give me part of the syrup. Rations were scare then and a taste of good ribbon cane syrup was mighty good.

"Well, he agreed to let me make the syrup on shares and while I was cutting down cane in the patch, General Lee and his staff rode by. I never saw a handsomer man, nor one so neat and fine looking. He sat on his horse as straight as an arrow, and his white beard made him look like somebody, I can tell you."

The old soldier sat up straighter in his chair at the recollection. "The men stopped and the General asked me what I was doing. I told him I was cutting the man's cane for him and was going to make syrup on shares for him. He looked at me and then he said, 'Go ahead, but be honest. Whatever you do, be honest with the man.'"

Mr. Tennille sat lost in thought for a few moments, then he shook his head and said, "He was a wonderful man, the boys would have followed him anywhere." And he wiped away a tear which stole down his cheek. Then with an obvious effort, he controlled his emotions and added, "General Lee rode with his whole foot in the stirrup, not just his toes like I had seen men ride. He had his foot in the stirrup clean up to here." And he indicated the point where the heel became a part of the shoe.

"He had open stirrups, not covered ones, and they were brass and shone like gold and his horse was so clean and pretty. I tell you he was a handsome sight."

"When did you join the army, Mr. Tennille?"

"Just as soon as there was any to join. I was a part of the Sandersville (Georgia) Volunteers and we started out in April, '61. We were part of the 28[Th] Georgia Regiment under Colonel D. J. Worthen, from Washington County and they sent us right up to Griffin to train awhile. Then we were sent to Manassas Junction and spent the winter there."

"Tell the lady about the time you ran from the Yankees," interposed a friend who had accompanied me on the visit.

"Well, if she wants me to tell the truth, I'll have to put something in about running away from them for I sho' did run one time. I remember when I went to school with Gus Avant, he could outrun me a longsight. But that time when we had to run, I left him a hundred yards.

"We were on picket duty, a line of pickets in holes dug out about three feet deep and six feet long, with the dirt thrown up on them to make breast works. Well, we saw the line of Yankees was coming to charge us and I tell you we left out from there. We saw Yankees over yonder and over here and that's when I outran Gus. Why, they were pouring 'minnie balls' at us and the bullets whizzed by me so fast, I could have caught a hatful if I had held out my hat. It's like that time Judge Calhoun asked a man if he ran at the Battle of Cold Harbor. He said 'Yessir, Judge, I show did run. Them that didn't run are there yet.'

"I was in the brigade of Alfred Colquitt who was afterward governor of Georgia and I was in Longstreet's Corps. I tell you there were more dead men that day at Cold Harbor than I ever saw in my life. There was a little branch there and the men had built breastworks along the line. The Yankees charged us 10 times that morning between daylight and 10 o'clock. And there were so many dead men, I could have walked from my house to Milledgeville on dead bodies.

"That was the day I killed a man. He is one of the few men I ever knew I killed in the war. I hate to talk about it but I reckon I can tell you. He started toward me and said he wanted to surrender. I told him to put down his gun and come on then and give up. But he suddenly cursed violently and started to shoot at me. I shot him then and he fell right in his tracks.

"It was three days before I got a chance to see him and try to find out something about him, there were so much fighting. But I went back to his body and found he had on a silver ring with his name on it and his company. His name was Michael Owen and he belonged to Company K, 155th of New York."

Mr. Tennille paused and was silent for a long time. He held up his left arm for me to see, then, and pulled back the cuff of his shirt sleeve to reveal a deep dent just above the wrist. "I got that at the Battle of Seven Pines," he told me, and then to his daughter, "Bring the bullet here and let them see it."

She quickly returned with the soft lead bullet, which had been taken from the arm of the young soldier 68 years ago.

"It did not do so much damage. I think it was a spent ball or it would have gone all the way through instead of sticking in my arm. I always have been sure that the bullet was meant for Captain Bob Flournoy. He was from Sandersville and was in charge of my company then. He was right next to me, running forward and he had his sword up waving it and flashing it in the sunlight. I know the Yankees were shooting at the sword when they hit me.

"I didn't exactly talk to the Lord when I looked down and saw the blood streaming out of my arm, but I thought about Him a heap. It didn't hurt, it just felt like it was dead, like I had no arm at all, and blood was pouring over everything. I reckon the main thing I thought about was how to get back home.

"I walked seven miles back to Richmond that night and I reckon I drunk a quart of whisky on the way, too. The ladies in Richmond were coming out in their carriages to take care of wounded men and when they met a stretcher bearer, they would take the man in the carriage and hurry him back to the city to the doctor. But the men who could walk, they just gave a drink to them and let them walk on.

"I stayed in the hospital in Richmond for a few days and then got a furlough and came on back to Tennille and walked over to Sandersville."

The grandfather of Mr. Tennille was Francis D. Tennille, a Revolutionary hero, who settled in Washington County and who gave the land for the right-of-way of the Central Railroad when it was run through that district. In consequence, the station was named Tennille, and most of the family lived in Washington County until after the War Between the States.

"Did you ever engage in battle with Negro troops?" I asked him.

"Yessum, I fought the later years of the war in Florida. I remember a Macon man was down there, too, a Mr. C. C. Anderson, who was long an engineer in Macon. (The man referred to is the late father of W. T. and P. T. Anderson.) We killed a heap of them, too, but not so many as the dead at Cold Harbor. It was a rich fight for me down there. I was barefooted and broke, hadn't been paid any money in a long time. I got a good pair of boots off a dead Yankee and $25.00 in good green backs and a pair of field glasses. I sold the glasses for $8 and that was the most money I had seen in a long time."

"You went back again, then, after you were wounded at Seven Pines?"

"Yes, ma'am. I was wounded the 31st of May in '62 and was home for about six months and then went back for the rest of the war. I was wounded again but not badly hurt and got a furlough. A bullet hit me a glancing blow between the eyes. Made me sort of sick and made my eyes mighty red and hurt for a long time, but I never did stop."

He paused again and a sudden recollection struck him. He chuckled. "I reckon I never was as bad scared at bullets as I was at a mule one night. Dick Lawrence and I were marching along pretty near sundown one night and we hadn't had much to eat in a couple of days. We saw an old rooster in the top of a barn. It was one of these old barns with a high top and there were poles sticking out all around it and pumpkins on all the poles.

"Dick told me if I would watch he would get that chicken and we would eat once more. So he climbed up after him. There was an old mule in that barn and when Dick had the rooster and started down, he tuned a pole somehow and all the pumpkins started rolling down. They hit that mule and he started kicking. I never heard such a fuss in my life. I bet I was more afraid than I ever was in battle."

He laughed the rather cracked laughter of old age, but his faded blue eyes reflected his enjoyment at the telling of old times.

"I remember another time I got shot at, but I was scared then. A man near our camp had a whole lot of potato hills and he had asked for a guard round it. Well, we were mighty hungry for sweet potatoes, so we fixed it up, with the guards, that we would give them some of the potatoes if they would promise to let us steal them. They would shoot but they were to promise not to shoot very straight. We managed to get away with a good bit of the 'taters all right. They didn't do much shooting till we got them.

"But the funniest thing we ever heard of a soldier swiping was one time when we were marching and we passed a place where there was a lot of bee gums. They were right under the window and we were all scared to try to take the gums. There was a man in my company who had raised bees and he knew all about them, so he told me to go and bargain to buy some meal and syrup from the folks and he would get the honey.

"Well sir, he stole the whole bee gum and carried it off with him and he never got stung once. The bees all poured out of the hive and settled right back where he took them from, and we carried the hive with us a few miles and I tell you I never felt like it was wrong. We had to eat."

"Were you often short of food?"

"Well, I don't know that I can say we were so short. The longest I ever went without anything to eat was three days and nights. We were in the Peninsula March, from Williamsburg over to Richmond. We had fought a little engagement at Williamsburg and the wagons were on ahead of us and we were making a forced march. I was barefooted and it was cold as rip and I had had no food for three days. I just thought I couldn't go any further. I sat down and said to myself I didn't care. I'd just let the Yankees get me. I was sitting there about to freeze and hungry as a dog, when Dr. Mathis, the brigade surgeon, came along. He was from Sandersville, too, and I knew him. He stopped and asked me what was the matter.

"I told him I was too hungry and worn out and I was just going to stop. He opened his knapsack and took out a piece of bread about as big as my hand and gave it to me. I gulped it down in about three swallows and just as I finished I looked up and saw way off yonder, the Yankees coming. I could see that long blue line. And I hit the grit."

He chuckled. "I forgot all about being cold or hungry or anything. I didn't want to be killed or captured."

"Were you ever captured?"

"Yessum. But I didn't stay captured long. We fooled 'em. It was on the Weldon Railroad, over close to Petersburg, Virginia. We had no artillery and they did. Well, they took about 25 of us and started marching us along and got lost. We didn't know any more where we were than they did. But we knew we had no artillery and they did not know it. So when the guns began sounding, we told them they were taking us the wrong way, that they were going right straight to our lines. We said we recognized our batteries.

"They didn't know we had no guns, so they believed us and turned round and marched us right back into our lines."

Mr. Tennille stopped to enjoy the situation all over again. When he had laughed enough, he went on with a broad smile still playing over his face. "When they took us, a Yankee wouldn't let me take time to get my hat and marched me away bareheaded. But I got even with him. When we marched back into our own lines, I took his hat. It was a good one, too, a heap better than the old one I had."

The veteran told of the times when the two lines were encamped so close together that men declared armistices and met halfway between the lines to swap tobacco for coffee. He talked about the rifles, which the sharpshooters used, the Glove rifles, equipped with sights which were somewhat like a telescope, drawing the far off object in effect very close up to the man armed with the rifle. He talked of his fighting in South Carolina and his walk home from North Carolina after the surrender.

But the most moving story of them all was the one concerning his comrade who was court martialed. It was a real effort for him to tell the story. He was obviously very moved and could not restrain his tears over the shooting of his close friend who had fought beside him for many months.

"He ought never to have been shot. He was as good a soldier as ever was. And the war was almost over too. We had a new commander in charge of us and he was different, so hard and tight on the boys. The discipline was being relaxed toward the end of the fighting and we were not used to being so tightly managed.

"One night we got paid off, the first money we had had in many a day. The commander went off and got sort of drunk himself. All the boys went out of camp for a holiday. When the commander came back and found so many men gone, he was very angry. He was drunk too and fighting mad anyway. He ordered the guard redoubled about the camp and gave orders to catch every man and demand his pass.

"There were about 150 men caught that night. They were tied up and waited to be judged. We were not used to any such doings and we would not stand for it. We were willing to fight, but we did not see why a man could not have a little fun now and then.

"So the rest of us charged the prisoners and released them all. This poor friend of mine happened to be one who was caught as the prisoners were getting away. He was tried by the court martial and sentenced to be shot."

There was a long pause and the aged soldier struggled with his emotions, but he could not stop the tears. They flowed silently down his wrinkled cheeks and onto his white moustache.

With a great effort, he continued his story.

"I was detailed as a member of the firing squad. Twelve of us with rifles, six of them containing blanks, stood a few paces away and fired at him. I have always believed that mine was the bullet which brought death to as good a soldier as ever wore the gray."

―――――――――――

Macon Telegraph, 1931, re-published by the Milledgeville (Georgia) *Union-Recorder*, April 22-24, 2000.

FIVE LIVING GENERATIONS
DWELL IN PIO NONO HOME

A great, great grandmother is "Aunt" Maria Grant, Negress, who lives with four succeeding generations of her matriarchy, on Pio Nono Avenue. Her age is only to be guessed at, for she was "nev'r tole endurin' de slavery times" and she knows only that she was grown, married and had three children when the slaves were set free at the close of the War Between the States.

Little and bent, her kinky hair white, her shriveled black skin a little dry and wrinkled, she is yet active and rules the house as if her daughter, Ella Stewart, who is a great grandmother herself, were still a child and her granddaughter, Cornelia Whittaker, who is a grandmother, were only a babe in arms. Poor Aleck, the great grandson, probably has no recognizable status and the babies who are of the fifth generation exist only to be petted by "Great Great Grand Ma.

"Aunt" Maria thinks that Ella her daughter, "must be about 60 years old," for she was born before the slaves were set free. "Ella wo'ies me er heap cause she hard er hearin'. I don't love ter holler and whoop at nobody," she said.

But "Aunt" Ella is serene and her appearance indicates that nothing "wo'ies" her. Mulatto in coloring, her hair white and almost straight, she sat on the door step and smiled and shook her head at all the questions asked her. She wrapped her old shawl a little more tightly about her shoulders when the breeze lifted it and huddled herself against the sunny side of the wall to keep warmer. But neither mother, nor grandchildren nor children bothered her.

Cornelia Whittaker, who was formerly Cornelia James and is the mother of Aleck, is 43, she thinks. She is tall and straight and unlike her elders, has long straight hair which she wears in two braids on each side of her head. She washes for some of "the white fokes" and "cleans up" for some of them, not having to bother about her motherless grandchildren while their father is working, for there are two more grandmothers to take care of them.

"Where did you come from, Aunt Maria? Were you born in this county?" the matriarch was asked.

"Naw'm, I come from Lee County, but I wuzen't bawn there. I wuz bawn in Putmon County. I belonged to de Newsomes in Putmon. Ole Man Johnnie Newsome was my old marster. We live twixt Sugar Creek and de Oconee River."

"Was that the place people used to call the 'Devil's Half Acre'?"

"'Naw'm!" she exploded. "Devil's Half Acre? Naw'm; won't no devil wid me. I show didn't live on no Devil's Half Acre. I hearn tell er it, but I didn't live in it."

"Do you remember about Sherman's march through Georgia?"

"Yessum, I hearn tell uv it, but I wuzn't there. I had done gone down to Lee County to live den. My old marster give me ter de young fokes. Mr. Joel Newsome wuz my young marster and he had moved down ter Lee County. My young mistis started me ter cookin' when we moved down there an' I been cookin' ever since."

"When the slaves were set free, did you leave your master?"

"Yessum. I had ter. Dey couldn't hardly take keer deyselves, let er-lone take keer er me an' my ole man and my chillluns."

Aunt Maria was a little reticent about her slave days. Perhaps because she is growing too old to recall very well the times of long ago; perhaps because she did not want to talk about them.

"Were you treated kindly by your young master?"

"Yessum, dat I wuz. I never hearn nothin' 'bout no bad treatment uv any my marster's crowd." She dropped her white head upon her hands and was quiet for a moment. Then she said:

"I see heap harder times now than I ever seed in my life. Endurin' er de slavery times, ev'y body had plenty ter eat and clothes ter keep warm. Us chillum used ter play in our shirt tails in de summer time— some time we went buck necked, jes es necked as my hand, but in winter we had warm clothes ter wear and we always had plenty ter eat.

"My mother worked in de fiel' an' we et in de white fokes kitchen an' we had plenty, too. White fokes was raisin' nigger chillun in dem days." She looked shrewdly at her visitor to see if she comprehended this last remark.

"Dey wanted ter raise as many chilluns as dey could so they'd have plenty uv 'em ter give ter de own chilluns."

Aunt Maria is a "saved and sanctified" Christian; she sees visions and has dreams of the other world. "I can't read," she explained. "I 'sperienced all I know. But I know I'm goin' ter heaven. I done been there once an' I'm er goin' ergin."

"When did you go to heaven and what did it look like?"

"Nemmine!" She shook her white head. "Nemmine. I ain't tellin' ev'y thing I know. But I wint up there one time. I seed my bowels wuz witherin' and I seed 'em spring up ergin lak green grass. I bleeved so strong in de Lawd and His promise, He carried me ter look on de other land.

"I had got religion but I kep' er grievin' erbout bein' saved an' look like I see a tree. I ax de Lawd how quick kin I clim' dat tree ter heaven. An' de Lawd took me up in a streak o' lightnin'. I look down on dis worl' and it was dark as night. But it was bright an' shinin' up there."

She looked at her visitor inquiringly. "Honey, if you ain't got 'ligion, you don't know nuthin'. De Lawd kin do anything. I heared a white lady sing er song whin I wuz a little gal—an' dat been long time ergo. Long time atter that I got religion an' I ax de Lawd ter tell me dem words dat lady sung an' de Spirit bring 'em ter me."

In her feeble cracked old voice she sang, "Come ter Jesus, as you air, weary an' worn an' sad." Then she faltered. Evidently the spirit could not help her remember the words.

After a while she laughed and dismissed the subject. Then she sighed. "I didn't want ter come up here to live. I wanted to stay in Lee county. But I had ter come. I show miss my church down there. I been goin' to this church here, the Missionary Baptist Church, but I miss my old church."

When her visitor left her, "Aunt Maria" was cuddling her youngest great great grandchild in the warm autumn sunshine, and singing to him in her cracked voice:

"I come to Jesus as I air, weary and worn and sad
I found in Him er restin' place uh-m uh-m uh-m-m-m-m."

Macon Evening News, Friday, October 23, 1931

FIVE SISTERS LEAD PIONEER LIVES

JACKSON SISTERS

This is the day of equal rights, but there are few women who really want the rights and privileges enjoyed by the "Jackson Girls," five maiden sisters who live near Hillsboro, Georgia, and who have done all the plowing, rail splitting, harvesting, planting, wood cutting and stock feeding, as well as the milking, cooking and washing for many years. Just how many it is hard to say, for since their father went away to the War Between the States, there has not been a man on the place.

The eldest is 83 and the baby is 73, and they are all active and able except the eldest, who had a stroke a few months ago and spends the greater part of her time in a rocking chair.

After driving down a dozen different roads, in vain effort to locate their house, I came upon a group of Negroes digging a grave in a lonely county churchyard and prevailed upon one of them to ride on the running board to show me where to turn off. He rode a mile or two, showed me a path which rambled through an old field, twisting and turning to avoid the pine trees and stumps, and told me to "drive rat on down dat road wen her gits ter Mistah Rich Garland's place, over dar bout half a mile, den you drive rat on pas' de house an' you see er tater patch on de lef', and de road forks rat dah. You takes de lef an' de white ladies lives bout er half er a quarter mile down de straight road."

Carefully following directions, lurching and bumping in second gear, dodging stones and trees and bushes, wishing I had taken the other rut, whichever one I selected, I finally arrived where lived the "Jackson sisters."

A rambling rail fence surrounded the place, the kind commonly known as a worm fence, and a gate, closed against intruders, was leisurely guarded by a large black hound dog. Bending over the wash pot in the front yard was an old lady with snowy hair, a dress which reached to the ground and an old-fashioned sun bonnet which completely shielded her face from the sun and observation.

She came at once toward the gate, shying a stone meanwhile at the dog in order to induce him to do his duty toward guarding the place from intruders. But on being informed to the nature of our visit and recognizing the Hillsboro lady with me as the daughter of an old acquaintance, she opened the gate and put the watch dog "at ease."

"Y'all come in," she invited hospitably and led the way onto a porch cluttered with boxes in which the dogs were wont to sleep, festooned with strings of red pepper, and decorated with various tin cans within which small green shoots struggled to bring beauty into a drab world.

"Rat in that room," she urged, and opened the door for us. We entered a large room, lighted only by the open door on the opposite side and the one which we had left open as we came in, for the only window was shuttered by a heavy wooden blind and was minus any sort of sash or window glass.

The pine floor had been washed white with many scourings and the two beds which stood in opposite corners of the room were beautiful examples of furniture of a generation agone: one a spool bed, the other a hard-carved four-poster, and both were adorned with coverlids of hand-woven beauty which made me gasp.

Seated in her chair before the whitewashed fire place was Miss Juliet the eldest, partially paralyzed, patient and sweet. She is a pretty old lady with a face remarkably free from wrinkles and a skin which showed clearly that she was a beauty in her younger days. Her hair is not very gray, despite her three score and twenty years, and it was easy to see that her sisters gave her patient and loving care.

Miss Lucy, for it was she who had met us, performed the introductions simply by saying, "Julie, here's some ladies come out to see us," and then she found chairs for us all.

Almost immediately, there entered the room Miss Marjie, herself, white haired and clad in garments which reached to her feet and were obviously home made and of the style of our grandmothers. In fact, the entire sisterhood scorns modern styles and the foolish fancies of fashionable dress.

In her mouth Miss Marjie wore a tooth-brush of the sort affected by snuff dippers and when she smiled, what few teeth remained showed unmistakably that I had made no error in bringing a present of a jar of "Rail Road Mills."

"Now, who be ye?" she said as she offered her toil-worn hand. I explained as best I could the reason for my visit and after surveying me curiously, she started from the room. I sought to detain her and she replied, "I aint got no time to be a foolin' long of you. I got to go out in the kitchen where sister is gettin' dinner. She is run down in her manner this morning and I reckon I better go help her a leetle."

I turned to Miss Lucy, the sweet-looking blond sister of 79 or thereabouts, who had met us upon our arrival. I asked her to tell me the names of all the family.

"I haint got much time to set here," she replied. "I got to git that washin' done. I aimed to git it done before 10:00 o'clock, but that old mule got out and I had to go fetch him and I sorter got behind."

Imagine it! Seventy-nine years old and doing the family washing! Not only that, but running down a recalcitrant mule.

Then she sat down upon the narrow boxed stair way which led to the attic and said, "What wuz it you're awantin' to know?"

"The names of your sisters and all about you," I replied.

"Well, I'll start at the oldest. Julie yonder, she's eighty-three."

And at once Julie interrupted. "I took the axe one morning an' went out to chop some wood and after I had been a chopping for about two hours, I come home and I couldn't hardly use this hand."

But Miss Lucy went on serenely. "Julie thinks that's whut brought on her stroke, but I tell her hit woulder happened anyway."

"The next 'un is Mary Anna Lizabeth, but we call her Betsey. She's the one out in the kitchen agettin' dinner." She then pointed toward herself with the finger of a work-hardened hand and said, "I'm Lucy. I come next, then ther's Marjie, that 'un whut jest went out er hare to the kitchen and Cynthie, she's the baby."

Cynthie sat in her straight chair near the door, which stood open and gave a glimpse of the back yard, and showed no sign that she heard her name mentioned. In her eyes was a look such as is seen only in the eyes of lonely mountain women or farm women, women who have been frozen by chill penury, who are like the man with the hoe, bowed by the weight of centuries.

The front door opened and Miss Marjie returned, followed by an old lady actually bent double with age and toil, her hair not yet quite gray and her eyes black and shrewd with the keenness of a mother tiger or an animal at bay, and her eyes did not belie her tongue for it, like the one Uncle Remus told about, "Knew no Sunday."

"Howdy," she said and the grip she gave my hand felt more like the grip of a woman of 18 than 81. Giving me a look that was embarrassing in its keen scrutiny, she asked abruptly, "You haint come here to make fun uv us, have ye?"

I hastily explained that I had come only to find out about their wonderful experiences, and their remarkable lives that I might tell others, saying, "I think it is wonderful that you five girls have lived here all these years without the help of any man and—"

But she interrupted proudly. "We haint need no man. I kin plow good as any man or split rails or do anything else ther's a needin' to be done. Least ways, I could before I got sorter old. I haint so much account now. I caint do no plowin' much, jest a little in my garden."

She looked at me with no hint of humor in her sharp eyes and added, "I bet you aint never done nuthin' like that. I bet you're a lazy sort of girl."

Laughing, I admitted the accusation, which Mrs. Sammons (who had accompanied me) said, "Oh, no, she is not lazy. She's one of the smartest women I ever knew."

"Well, I bound you she wasn't smart till she got Old-Man-Have-To behind her," asserted Miss Betsey vigorously.

Then changing the subject suddenly, she said, "You'll 'uv come ter a hospital here today."

"I'm sorry you are sick," I said.

"I haint sick, I'm jest down in my back today, jest sort of low in my body," she replied.

Miss Marjie, who was the best humored of the five, talking much and laughing a good deal, interrupted. "My back aint what hit ought ter be. I hurt it about four years ago and it aint been right since. I was going along leading the old mule an' a totin' a jug er water an' I caught my toe—that there'ns right there." She pointed to the toe of her left shoe—she wore men's shoes with broad toes and flat heels and laced up with a purple cord.

"I caught hit in one of these here roots, you know how they pull you. I kept a pullin' an' thinkin' it would turn aloose, and it wouldn't turn aloose, an' the mule kep' a pullin' an' the first thing I knowed it had jerked me down. My back aint been right since. Hit kept a gettin' worse an' I would er gone ter the doctor but I thought he couldn't do it no good lessens it was broke. I think I mighter jolted my kidney a loose.

"And another time I had put the mules in the pasture where they could graze and they got a nit fly after them an' they wuz running round an' takin' on an' I went to carry them to the spring ter water. Lucy was leadin' one, we finally got them to the spring an' the fly got after them again and that 'un Lucy had wuz cuttin' up so, I said, 'Lemme hold 'im,' an' while I was a taking hold er that bridle the one I had been er holin' hit me some way in the back. I aint never knewed whether he pawed me or bumped me with his head, but he hurt my back.

"An' another time, I wuz goin' to cut wood—no, let's see, I wuz a goin' ter the fiel' to haul some grass and the mule run over one of these deep gullies and dumped me in the road an' when they picked me up, I couldn't hardly breathe.

"An' another time—" But Miss Betsey interrupted.

"Staider holdin' on ter the lines, Marjie helt on te the side uv the waggin."

"I been workin' on the farm as long as you, mighty near," said Miss Marjie, a little hurt at the aspersions cast by Miss Betsey. "I dropped punkin seed before my paw went off ter war."

"We are all a getting sorter old now," said Miss Betsey. "We are so slow now it takes all day long ter git anything done. Take that fence out yonder. Hit's been a needin' fixin' fer the longest, but looks like we jest caint ketch up ter git to it."

Miss Marjie interrupted again. "I got a big load er manure needs ter be hauled out, but I cant lif' like I used ter could an' I been trying to get a Nigger to remove it for me, but he said after all these rains we oughter let the ground settle. I think it's plenty settled now, but they's a Nigger burin' in the neighborhood somewheres an' of course I couldn't expect to get any work done under the circumstances."

"That is such a pretty bed," said Mrs. Sammons, pointing to the spool bed, and Miss Marjie immediately retorted, "Paw bought that there set fer Julie when she was a growin' up."

Not to be outdone, Miss Betsey rose from her seat and walked across the room, her bent form swaying awkwardly. "I got the cheer my paw bought for me when I wuz a baby," she declared. "Hit wuz a rockin' cheer, but hit's been knocked around so much the rockers is done tore off. Old Man Ben Merritt made that cheer. It was painted green but the paint is all done wore off."

Proudly she displayed a child's size chair, hand-made and pretty with the severeness which characterizes furniture made by the pioneers. It was indeed worn smooth and devoid of paint from the handling of countless small fingers and the rockers were "tore away."

"Won't you get in it?" She turned to the little girl who had accompanied us and her face lighted up as it had done at nothing else since our arrival. The child, about three years old, went at once and seated herself in the chair, but she evidently misjudged the height of the seat and sat rather hard into it.

'Ef you wuz glass, you sho' wud er broke," laughed Miss Marjie, but she got no answering smile, save from the visitors.

"How old is that chair?" I asked Miss Betsey.

"Hit's near bout old as me," she responded. "I'm going on eighty-one and Julie's a goin' on eighty-three. Cynthie, there, she's the youngest and she is the gray-headest one of us all."

"Miss Julie doesn't look the oldest," I said. "She really looks like she might be the youngest of all."

Miss Julie smiled at the compliment and Miss Marjie laughed out-right. "She ought ter be the youngest lookin'," she said. "She aint got nothn' to do but jest sit in that cheer, the rest uv us got to work."

"Yes," Miss Betsey spoke up. "I took off eighty leetle chickens the other day an' when I went out to feed 'em they wuz five of 'em dead. A stinking old rat had cut through the board and dug a hole up under the coop. Hit had been a rainin' so the whole yard wuz in a loblolly, but I said 'doggone you, I'll fix you so you caint git in here again.' An' I got a hold er some slabs that somebody had sent here for us to burn and I cut a plank and fixed it."

"Yes," Miss Marjie put in, "we have worked the farm and done all there was to do, and then when it was rainin' and we couldn't work the farm, we wuz a standin' up spinnin' or weavin'. We used to do a heap uv that, but hit got so we either had ter give up the farm or give up the weavin'. Hit wuz jest too much an' I told Betsey that we'd jest have to leave off some uv it. As we couldn't give up the farm, it had to be done."

"That is certainly a beautiful quilt on the bed. Did you spin that?" I asked.

"That there aint no quilt, hit's a coverlid," said Miss Betsey in a superior manner, with a decided accent on the "lid."

"Well it is mighty pretty whatever it is," I said, and rose and went over to the bed to examine it more closely. "Did you dye the thread for it?"

The "coverlid" was a handsome square design of black and lavender upon a natural colored background and was woven with the art of a Roy Crofter.

"Course I dyed that thread," said Miss Betsey with her voice full of scorn for all who would buy thread already dyed.

"I bought the dye for that there purple, hit was this here analline dye or analeen dye whutever you're a mind to call it. But that black, I made myself out'n walnut hulls and He Pusley. You caint buy no black dyes that will hol'. They'll ev'r one fade out."

"What is He Pusley?" I asked.

"Haint you never seed no He Pusley?" There was unmitigated scorn in her voice. "You've seed Milky Pusley, aint you?"

I was obliged to confess I had not and she said, "You aint never seed much have you?"

I admitted it shamelessly and asked if I might see her loom, saying that I had never seen anyone weave and should like very much to watch her.

"You wouldn't know nothing bout it ef I was to show hit to you," she said. "You aint seed much. An I aint a going to git it. I bet ef I was ter come to yo house and want ter see something an' you wuz as tired as I am, you wouldn't want to git it."

I urged her, trying to be as good natured as possible, but she was adamant. "I aint a goin' ter git it nor they shaint," was final.

While Miss Marjie endeavored to explain to my untutored mind the intricacies of a seven-star quilt pattern, I let my eyes rove about the large room. Besides the two beds the room contained an old chest, nearly large enough for a coffin, the one rocker in which sat Miss Julie, seven straight chairs worn by time and much scrubbing to a smooth whiteness, and a small iron pot which sat in the corner beside the fireplace, obviously to heat water in. Over the door was a rude support made of branching hickory sticks, to hold the old fashioned muzzle-loading gun. Beside the back door was a "water shelf" with the usual country bucket and dipper and wash basin. Underneath them stood a little wooden truck of the yellow painted variety of the gay nineties. Hanging in one corner was a saw. The four steps visible before the stair turned to lead into the attic were adorned with plants in old buckets and boxes with snuff jars of varying sizes and with nondescript old pieces of quilts, clothing and such.

I came back from my survey just in time to hear Miss Betsey assert, "Thank God I am pore and thank God I was raised pore. I always have knowed how to work for my livin'. I aint able to do much now, but I have done a heap in my time.

"Our father left us in sixty-three and my mother died in seventy-one. After she died, there was some claimed we couldn't stay here, jest us five female girls with no man person. They wuz some talk about taking the youngest one and I told 'em they warn't a going to do it. Ma had give me that baby (pointing to the whitehaired 73 year old Marjie), and I warn't agoing to give her up.

"I aint able to work like I used to could. I didn't get the rest I need. I used ter wake up fo' day ev'ry mornin' but now I have ter wait for the chickens an' birds to wake me up. Some nights I don't git my rest. I don't git to sleep before 10:00 o'clock, I reckon."

"Did your father fight in the war?" I asked

"Yes, he wint ter the war and he never did come back. He died with the yellow janders up clost ter Dalton."

Trying to be polite and interested, I said inanely, "Well, I declare. Is that so?"

Leaning toward me with a rather angry look, Miss Betsey said, "You don' think I'm a telling you a lie do you?"

I hastily reassured her and she went on.

"I remember mighty well when the Yankees come here. The yard wuz jest a work with 'em. One of them officers told Lucy to go to the spring to git some water and she wuz skeered to go. He said, 'Why don't you go on?' I said to him, 'She's skeered, that's why.' And he tole her to go ahead and if any one of them Damnyankees bothered her he'd learn 'em how to bother her.

"So Lucy went and when she came back, she put the water inside the do', and I stood inside and reached the water to 'em in the gourd.

"Shaw! I seed them Yankee's when they wuz two mile from here. I said, 'The Yankees is a comin',' and Maw said, 'How ye know?' I said 'cause I see that fire birnin' over yonder.' The word had done been give out that they wuz comin. An' after a while, here they come, hollerin' and ridin' their hosses hard as they could. You could hear the water splosh in the creek half a mile off. I bet they rode them hosses across that creek in a lope.

"Paw had a fine stallion horse and they took that off and he had a filly with a colt and they took them too. They killed Ma's three turkeys and the chickens. An' I heared that over there at Mister Rich Garlands' house, they poured all the syrup out an' walked all over the house jest a poppin' groun' peas an' throwing the hulls on the floor."

Much more conversation followed about the mules "a getting out," how good the missionary s'ciety in Hillsboro is about helping them now that they were not so young as they had been, about folks who come there a wantin' to see things an' a tryin' to buy things but thank God they didn't have to sell nuthin' in their house yet, and folks wouldn't want to give half what they was worth anyhow, and finally a cordial invitation to stay to dinner, which indicated to me that it was time to leave.

So I departed amidst many invitations to come again and dark hints on their part that I would never do it. Miss Lucy insisted on opening the gate so's I could drive in the yard to turn the auto-mobelle aroun' and waved a kindly goodbye, but Miss Betsey was already back a gettin' the dinner and still low in her manners.

I drove away with my emotions in a turmoil as to which would gain the ascendancy; laughter over the amusing expressions, the pitiable conditions, sympathy for the gentle sister who sat so patiently in her chair of affliction, pain at the terrible tragedy of growing old and helpless. But overtopping all was my admiration for their courage, their hopefulness, their patient acceptance of the hardships which were theirs, their glory in it, the resentment they felt toward a pitying attitude and my large appreciation of the pioneer spirit which has enabled five women to make a living, however meager and pathetic it may be, out of the gullies and hills of a farm, and to be happy in spite of trials and hardships.

Macon Telegraph, ca. 1931

The Jackson Sisters of Hillsboro

APPENDIX I
A FEW FUN ITEMS

"lit a shuck" is a Southern expression for "getting out of Dodge REALLY fast."

* * *

Sue wrote a column about colons and hyphens on April 6, 1978, in which she said:

"The discussion brought back to me the story Margaret Mitchell told about hyphens. I spend a weekend with her in 1935 when she was correcting proofs for the forthcoming *Gone With the Wind.* She said she had "nearly gone blind" reading old newspapers to check for accuracy on historical facts she had used, and she "had nearly gone mad over the question of hyphenated words."

"For example, she said, in the proof the Macmillan Company had hyphenated the words "cape-jessamine" and "sweet-potato." The publishers had also tended to put in colons where she thought they were not needed. In exasperation, one day, she had sent the Macmillan editor a telegram in which she said she had "never liked colons, except gastronomically," but she would swap him "a colon for two hyphens."

(Look in your copy of GWTW and see how she came out in the argument.)"

* * *

Celestine Sibley, columnist for the *Atlanta Journal-Constitution* said:

"When Susan Myrick of Macon went to Hollywood to teach them how to speak Southern in the movie version of GWTW, it was her announced intention to ask for simple good English. The softness, the colloquial phrase gave it a Southern flavor with none of the mushiness, the whine, that sloshes around in less expertly done movies. Sue Myrick and her pupils did us proud.

* * *

Martha Kaplan, TV Teletime editor for the *Macon Telegraph*, wrote of the movie *North and South*:

"Southerners should genuflect at the mention of Susan Myrick's name. Only she, as technical advisor to *Gone With the Wind*, was responsible for that epic's Southern accents being palatable to the Southern tongue. *North and South Book I* pulled plenty of heat from states below the Mason-Dixon Line for its atrocious exaggerated Southern accents. ... Those movie folks need Susan Myrick."

* * *

A story handed down in the Myrick family from the time of the War Between the States about Susan's grandmother perhaps was the basis for a similar event in GWTW:

After the Yankee army destroyed furniture, burned the gin house, and took all the food and livestock, a cow somehow wandered back. Sue's grandmother milked the cow herself because the few slaves remaining, all old, would not do the milking.

* * *

Ground peas are peanuts.

* * *

He pusley and milky pusley are two of many varieties of purslane, a native, invasive plant. Some are edible.

* * *

Dorothy Parker's line: "Men seldom make passes at girls who wear glasses."

APPENDIX II

Liberty Hall, Alexander Stephens' home

Crawford Long House

APPENDIX III

Sherwood Anderson, a well-known writer in the 1930s, visited Sue and her friend Aaron Bernd when Margaret Mitchell was the guest of honor and spoke at the Macon Writers Club breakfast in 1936, shortly before GWTW was released.

Anderson stayed at Aaron's "country place" on that visit but did not go to the Writers Club breakfast. Sue wrote:

She was a witty speaker and convulsed her audience with her stories about the trials of being an author. But Sherwood did not hear her speech; he stayed quietly at Teeter, reading *Kneel To The Rising Sun*. But when evening came, Miss Mitchell, who was staying the night in Macon, came out to dinner at Teeter. During dinner, Sherwood was talkative and amusing, but later in the evening, when a dozen or so guests arrived and hung on every word Miss Mitchell uttered, laughing at the bon mots that fell from her lips, and encouraging her to carry on with her amusing chatter, Sherwood retired to a corner and sulked.

APPENDIX IV

"The Conquered Banner" and "Little Giffen of Tennessee" are two of the recitations Mitchell mentioned that are related to the Confederacy and the War Between the States.

The Conquered Banner
Abram Joseph Ryan (1838-1886)

Furl that Banner, for 'tis weary;
Round its staff 'tis drooping dreary;
Furl it, fold it, it is best;
For there's not a man to wave it,
And there's not a sword to save it,
And there's no one left to lave it
In the blood that heroes gave it;
And its foes now scorn and brave it;
Furl it, hide it—let it rest!

Take that banner down! 'tis tattered;
Broken is its shaft and shattered;
And the valiant hosts are scattered
Over whom it floated high.
Oh! 'tis hard for us to fold it;
Hard to think there's none to hold it;
Hard that those who once unrolled it
Now must furl it with a sigh.

Furl that banner! Furl it sadly!
Once ten thousands hailed it gladly.
And ten thousands wildly, madly,
Swore it should forever wave;
Swore that foeman's sword should never
Hearts like theirs entwined dissever,
Till that flag should float forever
O'er their freedom or their grave!

Furl it! For the hands that grasped it,
And the hearts that fondly clasped it,
Cold and dead are lying low;
And that Banner—it is trailing!
While around it sounds the wailing
Of its people in their woe.

For, though conquered, they adore it!
Love the cold, dead hands that bore it!
Weep for those who fell before it!
Pardon those who trailed and tore it!
But, oh! wildly they deplore it!
Now who furl and fold it so.

Furl that Banner! True, 'tis gory,
Yet 'tis wreathed around with glory,
And 'twill live in song and story,
Thought its folds are in the dust;
For its fame on brightest pages,
Penned by poets and by sages,
Shall go sounding down the ages—
Furl its folds though now we must.

Furl that Banner, softly, slowly!
Treat it gently—it is holy—
For it droops above the dead.
Touch it not—unfold it never,
Let it droop there, furled forever,
For its people's hopes are dead!

* * *

LITTLE GIFFEN
Francis Orray Ticknor (1822-1874)

This poem reflects the life of Isaac Newton Giffen, son of a
Tennessee blacksmith. By age sixteen Little Giffen had already been
involved in 18 battles in The War. Mrs. Ticknor, wife of the poet,
found the boy near death in one of the hospitals in Columbus, Georgia,

and took him to their home where he recovered. In March, 1865, when he learned that the Confederacy was about to fall, he left to join General Johnston. Little else is known of the boy other than he was killed in one of the closing battles of The War.

LITTLE GIFFIN

Out of the focal and foremost fire,
Out of the hospital walls as dire,
Smitten of grape-shot and gangrene,
(Eighteen battles, and he sixteen!)
Spectre! Such as you seldom see,
Little Giffen, of Tennessee.

"Take him—and welcome!" the surgeons said;
"Little the doctor can help the dead!"
So we took him and brought him where
The balm was sweet in the summer air;
And we laid him down on a wholesome bed—
Utter Lazarus, heel to head!

And we watched the war with abated breath—
Skeleton boy against skeleton death.
Months of torture, how many such!
Weary weeks of the stick and crutch;
And still a glint of steel-blue eye
Told of a spirit that wouldn't die.

And didn't. Nay, more! In death's despite
The crippled skeleton learned to write.
"Dear Mother," at first, of course; and then
"Dear Captain," inquiring about the men.
Captain's answer: "Of eighty-and-five,
Giffen and I are left alive."

Word of gloom from the war, one day;
"Johnston pressed at the front, they say."
Little Giffen was up and away;

A tear—his first—as he bade good-by,
Dimmed the glint of his steel-blue eye.
"I'll write, if spared!" There was news of the fight;
But none of Giffen. He did not write.

I sometimes fancy that, were I king
Of the princely knights of the Golden Ring,
With the song of the minstrel in mine ear,
And the tender legend that trembles here,
I'd give the best on his bended knee,
The whitest soul of my chivalry,
For Little Giffen of Tennessee.

INDEX

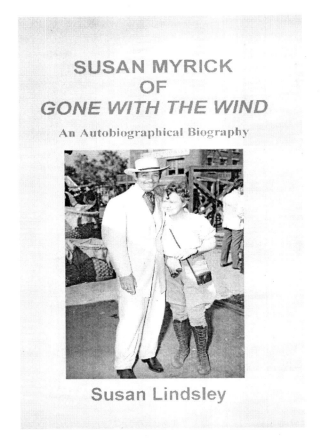

O YESTERPLACE AND OTHER POEMS

Return to your yesterplaces, to the times of banjoes at dusk, to Roy Rogers and Trigger, to the chapel down the lane, and other childhood memories. Here's the title poem:

O YESTERPLACE

O yesterplace, O yesterplace, my heart is there once more,
Dancing with the daffodils along the shadowed shore,

Walking in my yesterplace where music filled the air,
Banjos strumming in the night and laughter everywhere,

Rainbows in the summer sky and hayfields smelling sweet,
Ringing sound of horseshoes when we gallop down the street,

Crowing roosters in the dawn and hunting hounds at night,
Winter warmth beside the fire and kerosene for light,

Morning smell of biscuits and on Sunday, chicken frying,
Whippoorwills that fill the night with lonely, mournful crying,

Ghostly sound of childhood fears—a rustling in the wind,
O yesterplace, O yesterplace,
My heart is there in yesterplace and calls me home again.

$12.00 + $3.00 S & H

**From
Susan Lindsley
P.O. Box 33536
Decatur, GA 30033**

CPSIA information can be obtained at www.ICGtesting.com
Printed in the USA
LVOW08s0716200714

395093LV00001B/311/P